THE BEST IN POINT-OF-SALE DESIGN

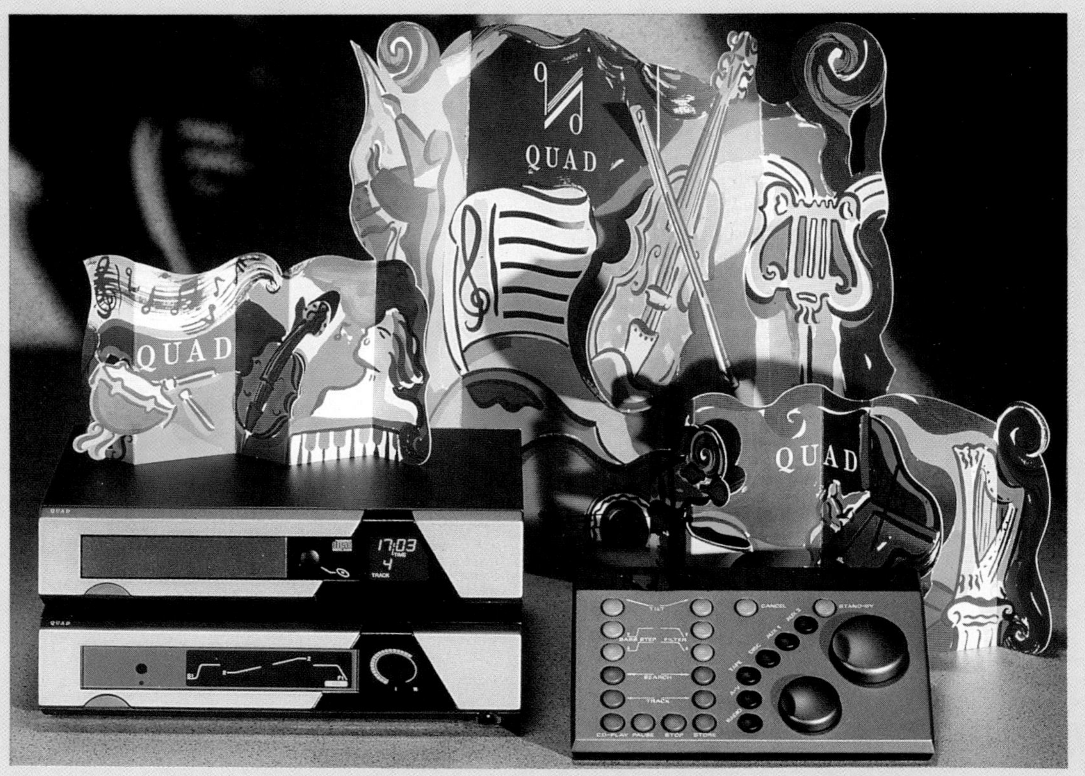
QUAD
QUAD
QUAD
17:03
TIME
4
TRACK
CANCEL
STAND-BY

THE BEST IN POINT-OF-SALE DESIGN

STAFFORD CLIFF

B.T. Batsford Ltd • London

A QUARTO BOOK

Published by B. T. Batsford Ltd
4 Fitzhardinge Street
London W1H 0AH

ISBN 0-7134-7395-9

This book was designed and produced by
Quarto Publishing plc
6 Blundell Street
London N7 9BH

Creative Director: Richard Dewing
Designer: Chris Dymond
Editor: Susan Berry
Picture Researcher: Michele Faram

Typeset in Great Britain by
Central Southern Typesetters, Eastbourne
Manufactured in Hong Kong by Regent Publishing Services Limited
Printed in Hong Kong by Leefung-Asco Printers Ltd

Stafford Cliff would like to acknowledge the help of the following people in the compilation of this book: Jeremy Schwartz, Fran Bell, Juliette Gouriat, Barry David Berger, Jonathan Scott, Stephen Paul, Alan McDougal, James Pyott, Bernard Dooling, Brian Wright and Bruce Heyhoe.

Contents

Introduction

Every brand manager and marketing manager knows the meaning of point of sale. A friend of mine, who works as a brand manager for a major chocolate manufacturer, defines it as promoting a product, "making the maximum use of the minimum amount of space, preferably using space in store that was not otherwise occupied, and preferably (in his case) as close to the till as possible."

Point of sale can be a much more cost-effective way of increasing product sales and, more importantly in times of recession, a much more definable and recordable way to spend the promotion budget than advertising or posters. And it is an area that is constantly changing, as new materials are developed and new products emerge.

Products such as video sales, which did not exist 10 years ago, are now one of the prime users of point-of-sale material internationally. With all this opportunity, why is it that point of sale still has such a bad image among designers? And why is it so hard to find good creative examples of the medium?

Poor relation A few years ago, if you asked a design company to undertake a point-of-sale project, you might be confronted by embarrassment and shuffling of feet, or, at the very least, you might detect slight nose-wrinkling as they ask if they can also tackle the brand identity or the packaging.

Compared with other areas of design, point of sale has always been the poor relation, often left to printers or packaging specialists, or the brand managers themselves. But with most of the Western world in the grip of a recession, design companies cannot afford to be so choosy. Clients spend less money on advertising – looking instead for a more immediate return on their investment. At the same time, retailers are looking at additional ways to move merchandise.

What is point of sale? A design team, working on a new retail concept, or the redesign of an existing store, will consider point of sale to mean all of the in-store graphics. High-level product identification, descriptive and directional signs, promotion and price ticketing, labelling on products, and shelf-edge signs might all be considered as some form of point of sale. And along with this comes the flexibility to move products around, change the look of the store seasonally, introduce sale and Christmas graphics, and marry the whole package to the exterior identity of the shop or, in some cases, the retail chain.

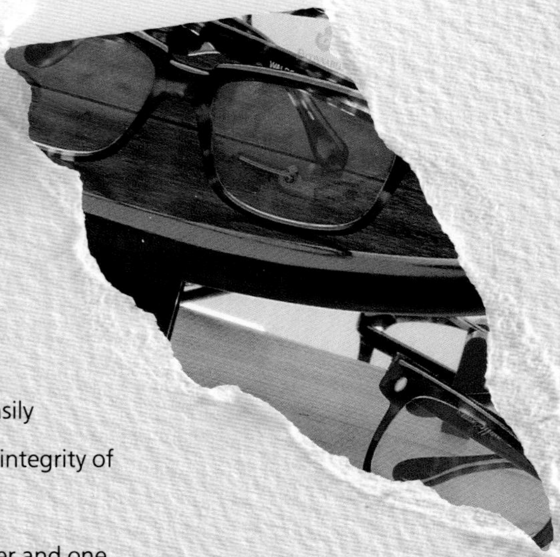

Point of sale, unless very carefully considered at the outset, can easily undermine (or even destroy) the image and unity of the store or the integrity of the product.

So we have two types of point of sale; one produced by the retailer and one by the manufacturer. A retailer who has spent a great deal of time and money creating and maintaining the look of his store will often not allow manufacturers or suppliers to use their own point of sale. But there is also a third type of point of sale, one which serves not only to promote the product, but to package and protect it as well. As costs of packaging increase and manufacturers and customers become more environmentally aware, they are looking at ways of combining the outer protective carrier of the product, with the inner display container or dispenser. In future, products sent to small independent retailers (where most traditional point-of-sale occurs) might arrive in packs that can be adapted, cut open or folded back to go straight into the shop.

The way forward This is a fresh challenge that will not be met by the graphic designer alone. It will take the skills of the manufacturer, the industrial designer and the package specialist to come up with new and truly innovative solutions.

As more and more manufacturers merge and combine, it is easy to imagine a time when a store will consist of only the basic shell – walls, lighting and, perhaps, signage. Shelving might comprise very basic fixtures, into which the manufacturers' own merchandizing modules would fit, adapted and tailor-made for each product.

This book is not a comprehensive survey of every type of point of sale that exists, or has ever been produced. It is a selection of the most interesting solutions to the widest possible cross-section of briefs, which I hope will provide inspiration to anyone about to undertake a point-of-sale project themselves.

Window display material Some of the most creative display work over the last 20 years has been done by large department stores, who employ their own teams of designers to think up and then implement ideas to promote their product lines, draw people into their stores, and entertain passers-by. Who, as a child, has not been taken window shopping to see the Christmas displays? In New York, large stores even commission named artists to create fashion windows, and roped-off areas are set up on the sidewalk to allow people to file past these mechanically operated "magic kingdoms". Even limitations of size are not a restriction – Tiffany's tiny windows have long been famous for their creativity and imagination.

But stores with more than one outlet, chains of franchises all over the world, or manufacturers keen to provide material to attract attention to their product in otherwise unimaginative low-cost windows, must resort to mass-produced solutions: cardboard cut-outs, printed posters, and photographic blow-ups are the techniques most often utilized in this sector.

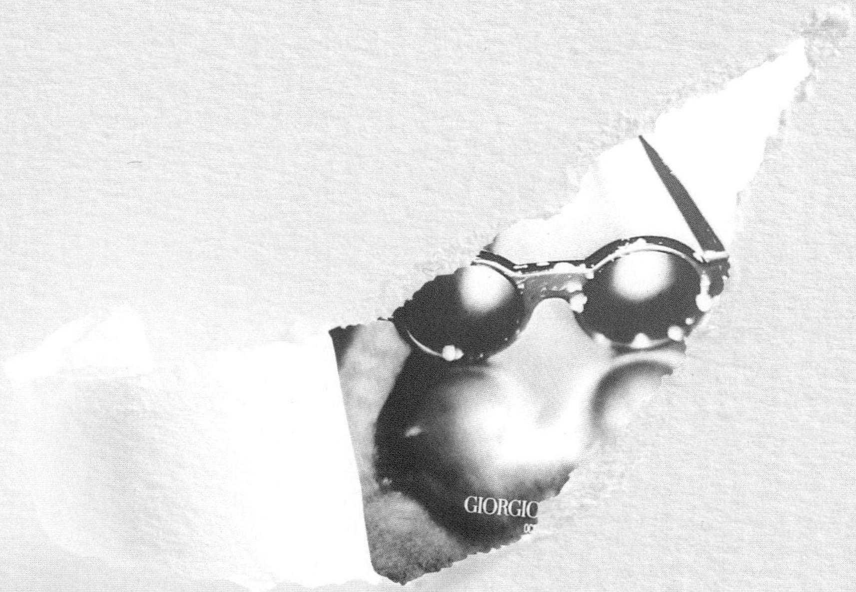

No.1
No.2

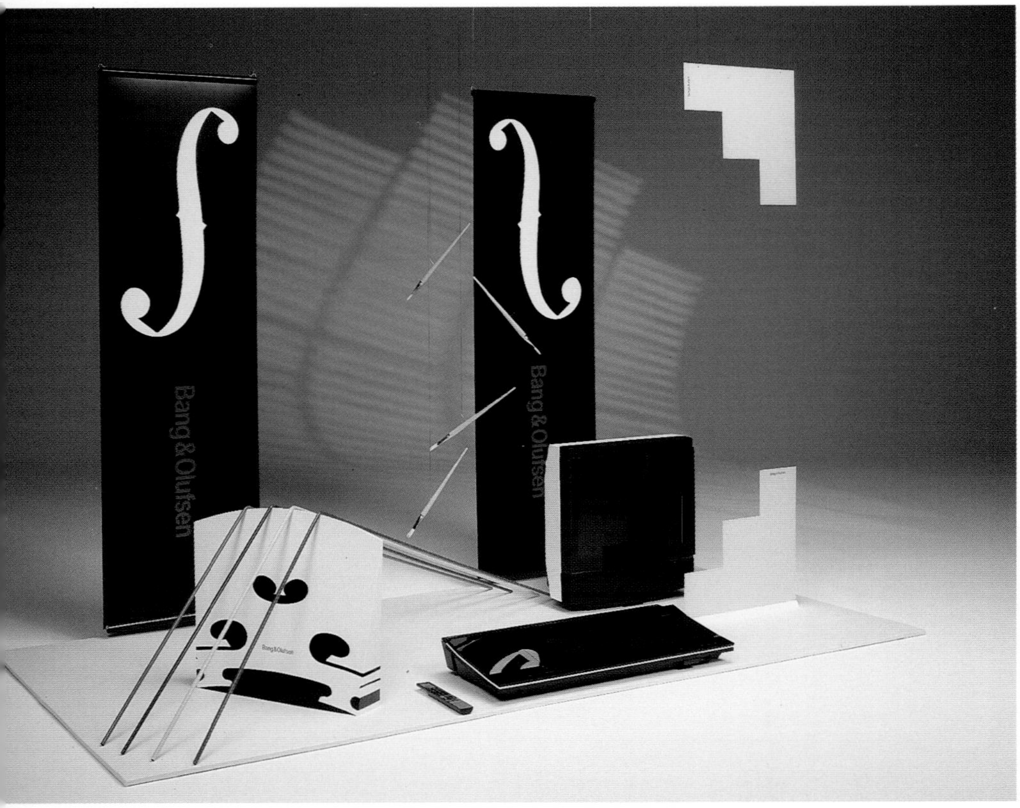

The Art of Painting

CLIENT: Bang & Olufsen A/S, Struer, Denmark

DESIGNER: Studio John Boye, Struer, Denmark

ILLUSTRATOR/PHOTOGRAPHER: Ib Sorensen

DATE OF COMPLETION: Spring 1991

TARGET MARKET: Europe, USA, Canada, Asia

PLACE OF SALE: Bang & Olufsen's distribution and organization

CLIENT'S BRIEF: A generic window decoration for adaptation during the season 1991/2.

DESIGN RATIONALE: Art elements – like the forms from bowed string instruments – signal music. Another element, like colour, is also often used – here in the colours of the spectrum as strings over the violin chair. The paint brushes are suspended on thin threads to look like mobiles. Two backdrops with graphic symbols from a viola are used to attract attention.

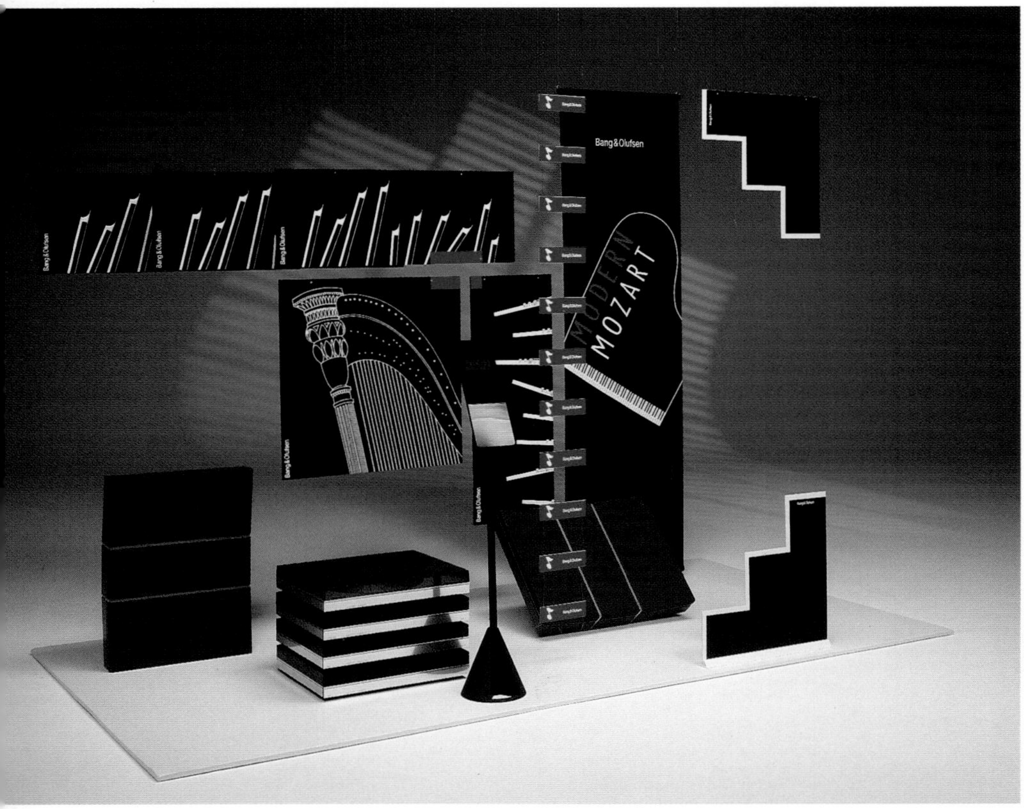

The Art of Music

CLIENT: Bang & Olufsen A/S, Struer, Denmark

DESIGNER: Studio John Boye, Struer, Denmark

ILLUSTRATOR OR PHOTOGRAPHER: Ib Sørensen, Struer, Denmark

DATE OF COMPLETION: Spring 1991

TARGET MARKET: Europe, USA, Canada and Asia

PLACE OF SALE OF PRODUCT: Bang & Olufsen's distribution and organization

CLIENT'S BRIEF: In connection with the jubilee year 1991 for Mozart's birthday, 'Modern Mozart' was chosen as the theme to emphasize that music is immortal. The window decoration follows a campaign with musical evenings all over the world with presentation of Mozart's music on Bang & Olufsen music systems.

DESIGN RATIONALE: Modern Mozart, but with old instruments. The theme was extended with the symphony as the visual concept. Instruments in pure graphic reproductions of black/white with the staircase element from the season. The window decoration is composed of several elements to make it adaptable for large and small windows.

The Art of Ballet

CLIENT: Bang & Olufsen A/S, Struer, Denmark
DESCRIPTION OF PRODUCT: Window display
DESIGNER: Studio John Boye, Struer, Denmark
ILLUSTRATOR OR PHOTOGRAPHER: Ib Sørensen, Struer, Denmark
DATE OF COMPLETION: Spring 1991
TARGET MARKET: Europe, USA, Canada, Asia
PLACE OF SALE: Bang & Olufsen's distribution and organization
CLIENT'S BRIEF: A generic window decoration for the season 1991/92.
DESIGN RATIONALE: Music in other art forms – like here in ballet, represented by a pair of feet and legs, which in a black/white print signal movement. The red bow at the bottom is another element from the ballet which together with the staircase signal "on the way up." The staircase is made of materials that can carry small products as shown on the illustration. Here terminals are shown for the operation of Bang & Olufsen products.

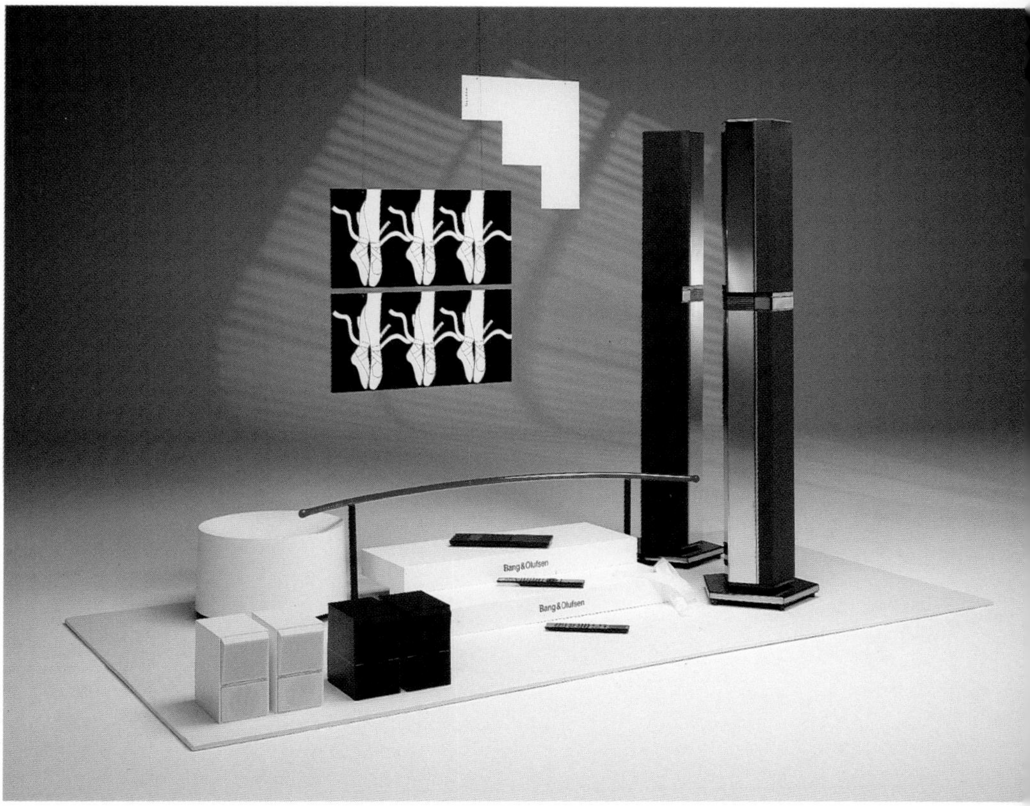

The Art of Christmas

CLIENT: Bang & Olufsen, Struer, Denmark
DESCRIPTION OF PRODUCT: Window display
DESIGNER: Studio John Boye, Struer, Denmark
ILLUSTRATOR OR PHOTOGRAPHER: Ib Sørensen, Struer, Denmark
DATE OF COMPLETION: Spring 1991
TARGET MARKET: Europe, USA, Canada, Asia
PLACE OF SALE: Bang & Olufsen's distribution and organization
CLIENT'S BRIEF: Christmas window – with symbols that clearly signal Christmas 91/92.
DESIGN RATIONALE: To create purchase bags in beautiful materials, printed with Christmas symbols. The bags are suspended on a light metal stand forming a Christmas tree. The same Christmas elements are hung as mobiles from the ceiling.

The Art of Writing

CLIENT: Bang & Olufsen A/S, Struer, Denmark

DESIGNER: Studio John Boye, Struer, Denmark

DATE OF COMPLETION: Spring 1991

TARGET MARKET: Europe, USA, Canada and Asia

PLACE OF SALE OF PRODUCT: Bang & Olufsen's distribution and organization

CLIENTS' BRIEF: A generic window decoration for adaptation to the whole 1992/93 season

DESIGN RATIONALE: The design language of Bang & Olufsen's window decoration often utilizes elements from the world of music, like the notes that signalize music and sound. The intention was to be able to extend the generic window from small to large windows.

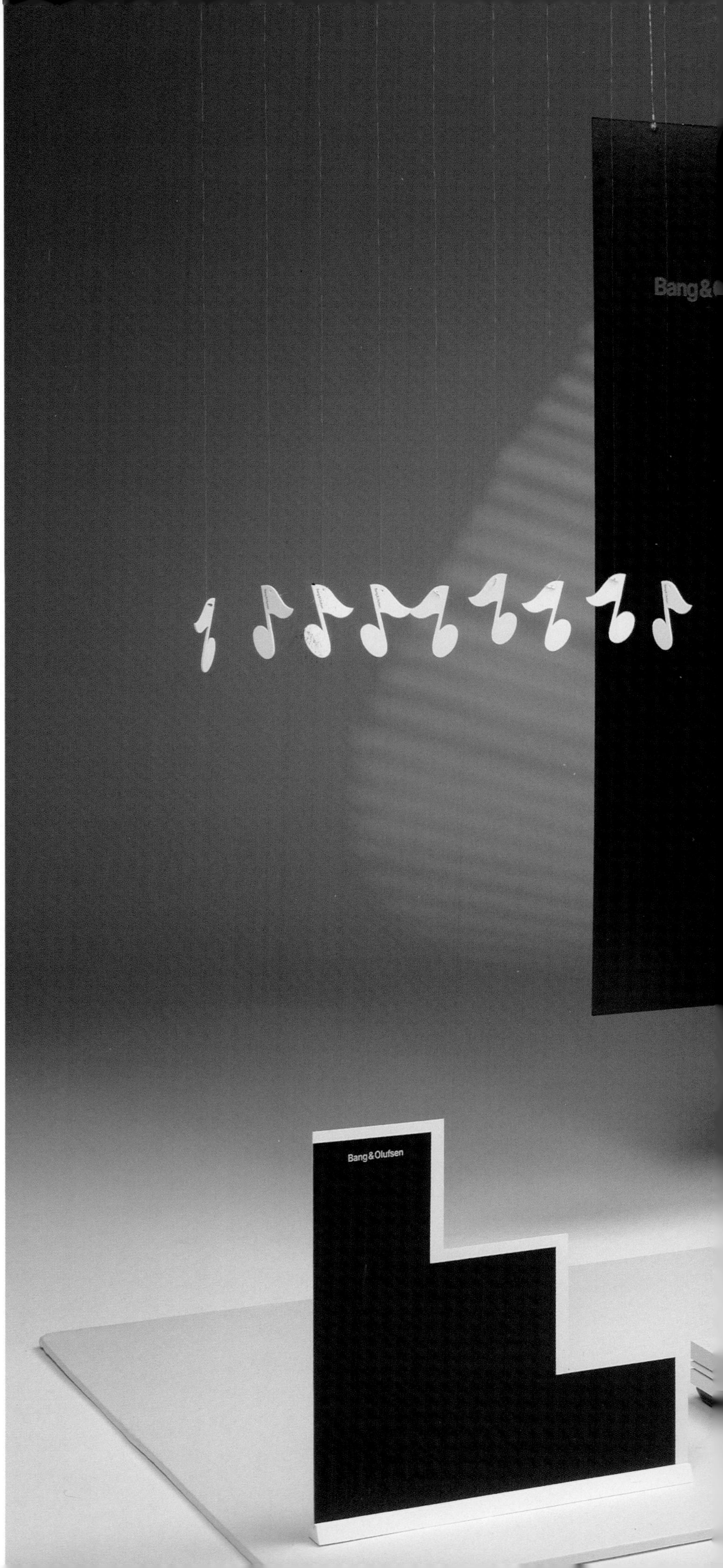

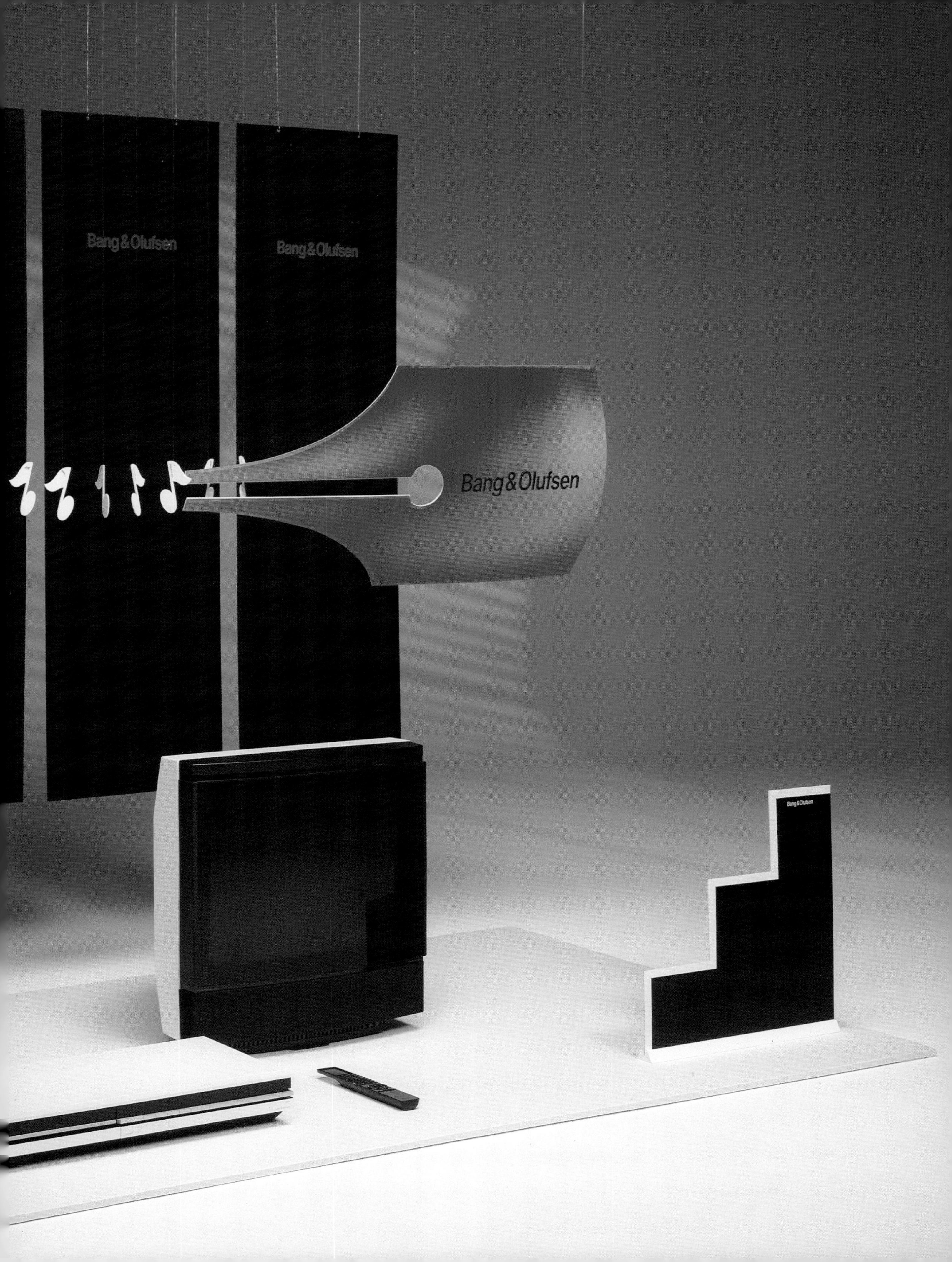
Bang&Olufsen
Bang&Olufsen
Bang&Olufsen
Bang&Olufsen

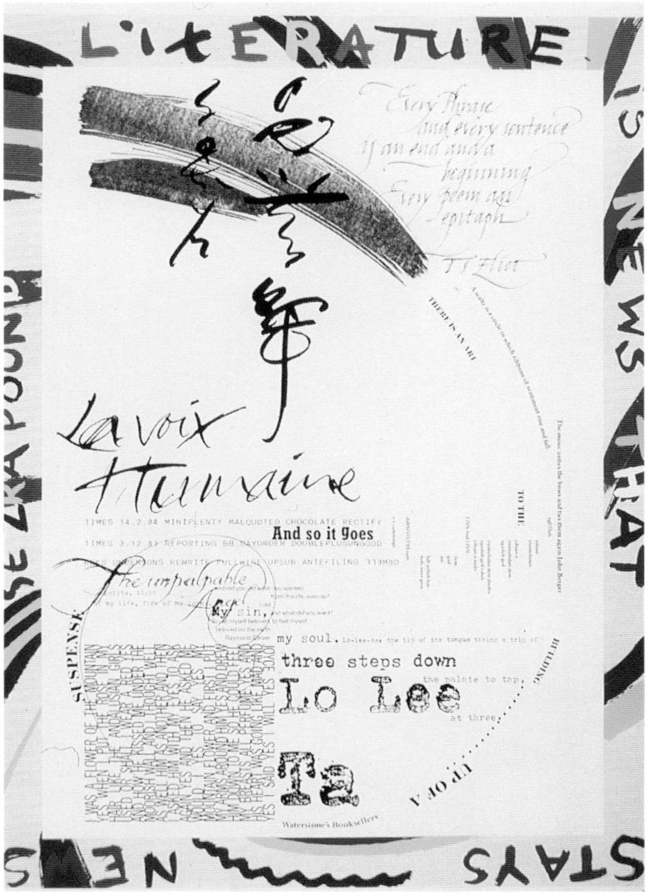

Book Posters

CLIENT: Waterstones Booksellers, London, UK

DESCRIPTION OF PRODUCT: Posters on subject themes – literature, travel, food, drink and gardening, architecture, history and classical art, modern arts, drama, philosophy and politics, Christmas

DESIGNER: Newell & Sorrell, London, UK

DATE OF COMPLETION: 1992

TARGET MARKET: Bookshop customers at Waterstone's retail outlets

A FEAST
CHRISTMAS FARE

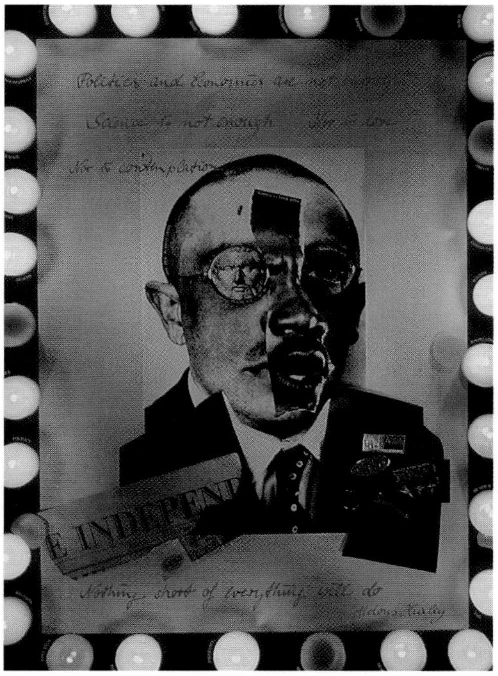
Politics and Economics are
Science is not enough
Nor is contemplation
E INDEPEND
Nothing short of everything will do
Aldous Huxley

NIL POSSE CREARI DE NILO

Christmas Banners

CLIENT: Sherratt & Hughes, London, UK (now merged with Waterstones Ltd)

DESCRIPTION OF PRODUCT: Banners, catalogue, bookmarks and gift vouchers for bookshop

DESIGNER: Newell & Sorrell, London, UK

ILLUSTRATOR: Alan Cracknell

DATE OF COMPLETION: 1989

TARGET MARKET: Book shop customers

CLIENT'S BRIEF: To create a range of point-of-sale material that would work on its own or as a set.

'Egypt' mortgage promotion

CLIENT: Bristol & West Building Society, Bristol, UK

DESCRIPTION OF PRODUCT: Window display and point-of-sale units for branch network

DESIGNER: Proctor & Stevenson, Bristol, UK

ILLUSTRATOR OR PHOTOGRAPHER: Sue Shields

DATE OF COMPLETION: 1991

TARGET MARKET: All potential mortgage borrowers

PLACE OF SALE: Building Society branches

CLIENT'S BRIEF: Initially to design a booklet explaining the full range of mortgage services. This brief was subsequently developed by Proctor & Stevenson.

DESIGN RATIONALE: To ensure that the booklet was actually read and to attract potential new customers. A competition was devised using the analogy of ancient Egypt with a series of graphic and written clues to win a holiday in Egypt for two. The prominent window displays, posters and point-of-sale attracted thousands of potential new customers into the branches.

Dillons Window Display

CLIENT: Pentos Retailing Ltd, Birmingham, UK

DESIGNER: Stocks Taylor Benson Ltd, Endersby, Leicestershire

ILLUSTRATOR OR PHOTOGRAPHER: Copyright-free images

DATE OF COMPLETION: February 1991

TARGET MARKET: ABC male/female, equal bias; 25–60 years old

PLACE OF SALE: Dillons the Bookstore and Athena Bookstores (approximately 100 outlets)

CLIENT'S BRIEF: To create a more theatrical and three-dimensional set of window display material that would be interchangeable throughout the spring season.

DESIGN RATIONALE: Great flexibility of items meant that card 'props' could be interchangeable and therefore maintain freshness. Columns and urns give a feel that is traditional and upmarket.

EASTER
d

Fuzzy Peach

CLIENT: Body Shop, London, UK

DESCRIPTION OF PRODUCT: Range of peach-scented products (perfume, soaps, etc.)

DESIGNER: Alan McDougall and Frances Myers, Body Shop

ILLUSTRATOR OR PHOTOGRAPHER: Tom Connell

DATE OF COMPLETION: January 1991

TARGET MARKET: Female, all ages

PLACE OF SALE: Window and in-store Body Shops

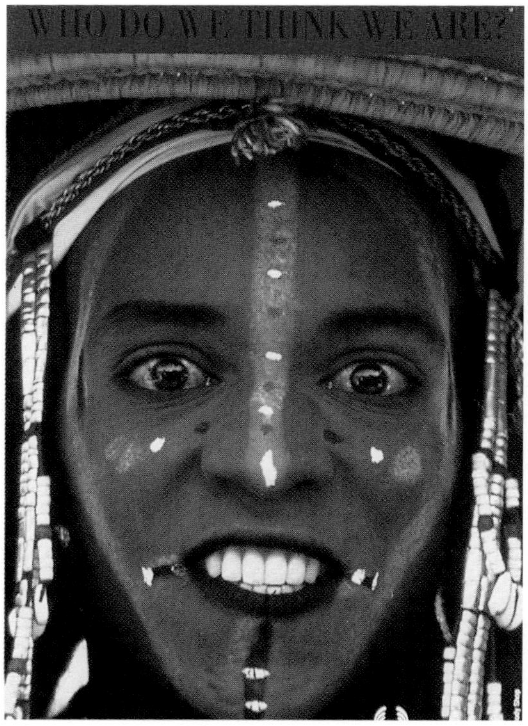

Who Do We Think We Are 'Millenium'

CLIENT: Body Shop, London, UK

DESCRIPTION OF PRODUCT: Anthropological book and TV series

DESIGNER: Frances Myers, Body Shop

ILLUSTRATOR OR PHOTOGRAPHER: Carol Beckwith

DATE OF COMPLETION: April 1992

TARGET MARKET: Male/female, all ages

PLACE OF SALE: Window and in-store promotion

DESIGN RATIONALE: To raise awareness of the plight of indigenous peoples around the world. To celebrate the diversity of cultures and what we can learn from them.

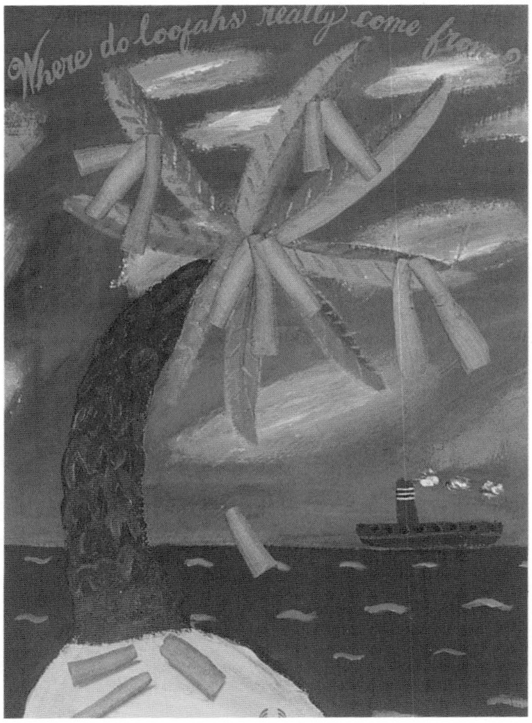

Where do loofahs really come from?

CLIENT: Body Shop, London, UK

DESCRIPTION OF PRODUCT: All Body Shop suncare products and sundry items

DESIGNER: Frances Myers, Body Shop

ILLUSTRATOR OR PHOTOGRAPHER: Christopher Corr

DATE OF COMPLETION: April 1991

TARGET MARKET: Male/female, all ages

PLACE OF SALE: Window and in-store Body Shops

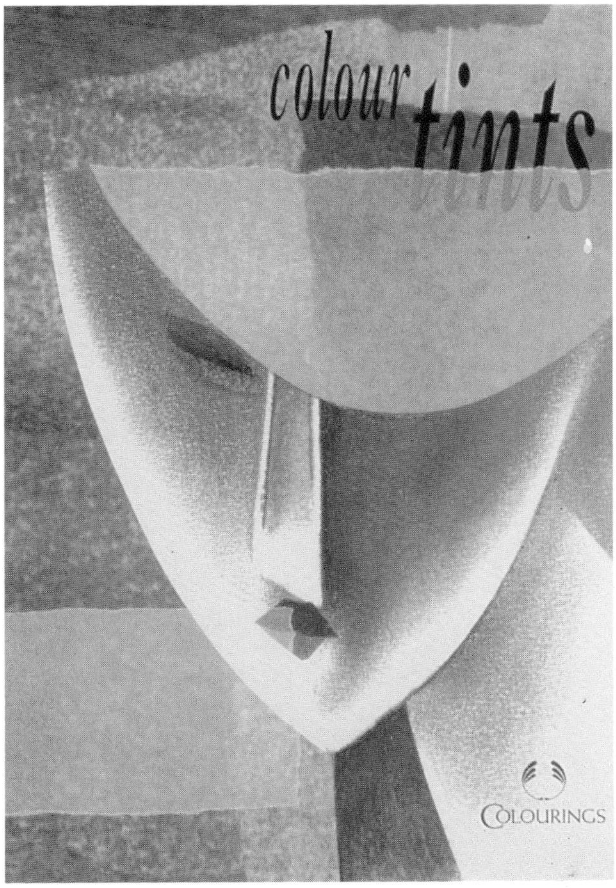

Colour Tints

CLIENT: Body Shop, London, UK

DESCRIPTION OF PRODUCT: Lipsticks

DESIGNER: Frances Myers, Body Shop

ILLUSTRATOR OR PHOTOGRAPHER: Frances Myers

DATE OF COMPLETION: February 1991

TARGET MARKET: Female, all ages

PLACE OF SALE: Window and in-store Body Shops

Cool Clean Cucumber

CLIENT: Body Shop, London, UK

DESCRIPTION OF PRODUCT: Cucumber cleanser and skin toner

DESIGNER: Frances Myers, Richard Browning, Debbie Littley, Body Shop

ILLUSTRATOR OR PHOTOGRAPHER: Tom Connell

DATE OF COMPLETION: February 1991

TARGET MARKET: Females/males, all ages

PLACE OF SALE: Window and in-store Body Shops

Extinct is Forever

CLIENT: Body Shop, London, UK
DESCRIPTION OF PRODUCT: Soaps and sundry items that heighten awareness that animals face extinction
DESIGNER: Frances Myers and Bertha Thackeray, Body Shop
ILLUSTRATOR OR PHOTOGRAPHER: Frances Myers
DATE OF COMPLETION: March 1992
TARGET MARKET: Primarily children and young adults
PLACE OF SALE: Window and in-store Body Shops
DESIGN RATIONALE: To raise awareness of plight of rare animals which are in danger of extinction. To promote range of products, especially among children, and encourage them to take action to help preserve animals in danger.

Complete Colour

CLIENT: Body Shop, London, UK
DESCRIPTION OF PRODUCT: Cosmetics that can be used to colour eyes, lips and cheeks
DESIGNER: Frances Myers, Body Shop
ILLUSTRATOR OR PHOTOGRAPHER: Ivan Alen
DATE OF COMPLETION: March 1992
TARGET MARKET: Female, all ages
PLACE OF SALE: Window and in-store Body Shops

Colour Correctives

CLIENT: Body Shop, London, UK
DESCRIPTION OF PRODUCT: Make-up to help disguise discoloured skin/birthmarks, etc.
DESIGNER: Frances Myers and Fionnuala Conway, Body Shop
ILLUSTRATOR OR PHOTOGRAPHER: Frances Myers
DATE OF COMPLETION: September 1991
TARGET MARKET: Male/female, all ages
PLACE OF SALE: Window and in-store Body Shops

Mostly Men

CLIENT: Body Shop, London, UK

DESCRIPTION OF PRODUCT: Male cleansing, shaving and bath products

DESIGNER: Frances Myers

ILLUSTRATOR OR PHOTOGRAPHER: Richard Spice

TARGET MARKET: Males, all ages

Cleanse, Polish, Protect Face

CLIENT: Body Shop, London, UK

DESCRIPTION OF PRODUCT: All Body Shop skincare products

DESIGNER: Alison Philpot, Body Shop

ILLUSTRATOR OR PHOTOGRAPHER: Alison Philpot

DATE OF COMPLETION: December 1991

TARGET MARKET: Male/female, all ages

PLACE OF SALE: Window and in-store Body Shops

Poster Series

CLIENT: Decca Record Company, London, UK

DESCRIPTION OF PRODUCT: Posters

DESIGNER: The Partners, London, UK

ILLUSTRATOR OR PHOTOGRAPHER: Various

DATE OF COMPLETION: January 1989

TARGET MARKET: Retail

PLACE OF SALE: Record shops

CLIENT'S BRIEF: Posters were to be part of a scheme to encompass the wide range of products that Decca sells.

DESIGN RATIONALE: The Partners took a disciplined approach to design in which strictly ordered typography and consistent visual elements made all posters, brochures and adverts instantly recognizable. For the posters, imagery was built up in layers to create visual excitement.

sir georg solti

kiri te kanawa
josé carreras
orchestra e coro del
teatro comunale di bologna
riccardo chailly

NIELSEN
HERBERT BLOMSTEDT
san francisco symphony herbert blomstedt
HINDEMITH
HERBERT BLOMSTEDT

Wilkes Bashford Spring '89 Visual Identity

CLIENT: Wilkes Bashford, San Francisco, California, USA

DESIGNER: Morla Design Inc, San Francisco, California, USA

ILLUSTRATOR OR PHOTOGRAPHER: Jennifer Morla

DATE OF COMPLETION: January 1989

TARGET MARKET: High-end men's fashion

PLACE OF SALE: Wilkes Bashford Department Stores, USA

DESIGN RATIONALE: For high-end men's fashion boutique. Leger-inspired illustration allowed for proper positioning of the varied Spring clothing line.

Armani Glasses

CLIENT: Giorgio Armani, Italy

DESCRIPTION OF PRODUCT: Acetate covered slip-case with photograph of glasses

DESIGNER: Maddie Bennett, London, UK

DATE OF COMPLETION: June 1989

TARGET MARKET: International market

PLACE OF SALE: Worldwide distribution

CLIENT'S BRIEF: To produce an international house style for Giorgio Armani glasses. The photographic image and simple typography combine to create a distinctive brand identity, endorsed with the quality of Armani.

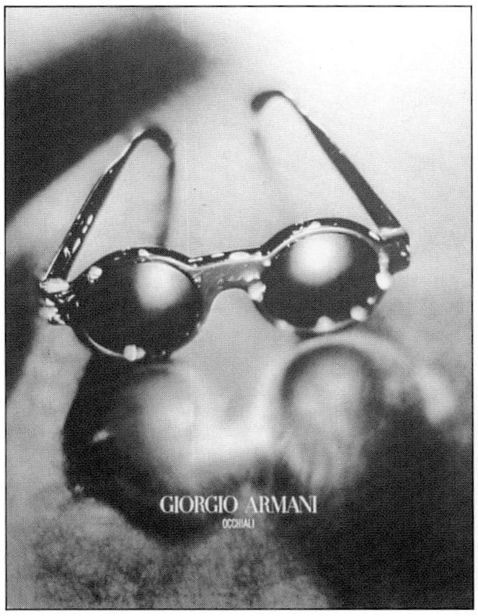

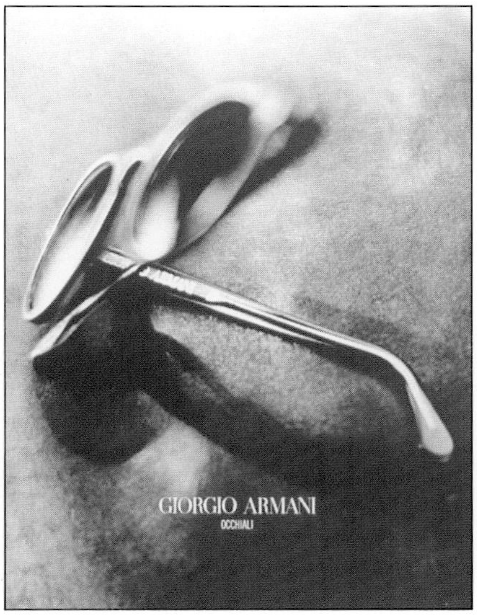

Dillons Christmas Display

CLIENT: Pentos Retailing Ltd, Birmingham

DESIGNER: Stocks Taylor Benson Ltd, Enderby, Leicestershire

ILLUSTRATOR/PHOTOGRAPHER: Stocks Taylor Benson Ltd

DATE OF COMPLETION: November 1990

TARGET MARKET: ABC male/female equal bias; 25–60 years old

PLACE OF SALE: Dillons The Bookstore and Athena Bookstores (approximately 100 outlets)

CLIENT'S BRIEF: To create attractive seasonal point of sale, primarily for windows, that could be carried through in-store.

DESIGN RATIONALE: A high-impact clown character was used to link all items by style and colour to create colourful yet traditional and sophisticated display graphics, appropriate to the target market.

MERRY
CHRISTMAS
MERRY
CHRISTMAS
MERRY
CHRISTMAS
DICKENS
Peter Ackroyd
REG
KRAY
BORN FIGHTER
JOHN
AHERN
MERRY
CHRISTMAS
MERRY
CHRISTMAS
Pick of
PUN
Edited by D
TERENCE
STRONG
Sons
of
Heaven
MERRY
CHRISTMAS

Peter Rabbit

CLIENT: Frederick Warne, Penguin Books, London, UK

DESCRIPTION OF PRODUCT: Cardboard cut-out, free-standing display piece (45 × 32cm)

DESIGNER: Frederick Warne, Penguin Books, London, UK

DATE OF COMPLETION: 1985

TARGET MARKET: Booktrade

PLACE OF SALE: Bookshops

CLIENT'S BRIEF: To design an eye-catching free-standing point-of-sale display piece using Beatrix Potter's *Peter Rabbit* character, incorporating a novelty element and remaining true to Beatrix Potter's original illustrations and style.

DESIGN RATIONALE: An interactive novelty style showcard was produced that enables Peter Rabbit to pop out of the watering can.

The Tailor Mouse

CLIENT: Frederick Warne, Penguin Books, London, UK

DESCRIPTION OF PRODUCT: Cardboard cut-out, free-standing display piece (45 × 32cm)

DESIGNER: Frederick Warne, Penguin Books, London, UK

DATE OF COMPLETION: 1985

TARGET MARKET: Booktrade

PLACE OF SALE: Bookshops

CLIENT'S BRIEF: To design a visually appealing free-standing display piece using Beatrix Potter's character *The Tailor Mouse*. It was important to remain true to the original illustration and style, and incorporate space for the display of a book.

DESIGN RATIONALE: An attractive showcard was produced using a cut-out of The Tailor Mouse. The book slot was positioned to look as though the character is holding the book, which is visually appealing and meets the requirements set out in the brief.

The Quad Hi-Fi Product Range

CLIENT: Quad Electro-acoustics Limited, Huntingdon, Cambridgeshire, UK

DESIGNER: Dinah Lone, RSCG Conran Design, London, UK

ILLUSTRATOR: Helen Manning

DATE OF COMPLETION: June 1991

TARGET MARKET: Music lovers

PLACE OF SALE: Independent hi-fi retailers and department stores

CLIENT'S BRIEF: To get the customer to focus on Quad products displayed alongside competitors' products either in the window or instore. The graphic display must work with stacked groups and individual products. It must be recognized as Quad without identifying individual products. An inexpensive, simple, high-quality solution, stressing the relationship with Quad and music.

DESIGN RATIONALE: Three display headers, two for positioning on top of the product and one behind; creating a 3-dimensional stepped effect. Each header comprises a single sheet of card, die-cut and scored. Delivered flat, they are simple to construct. Creative illustration depicting stylized musical performance is an integral part of the cut-out, folding design.

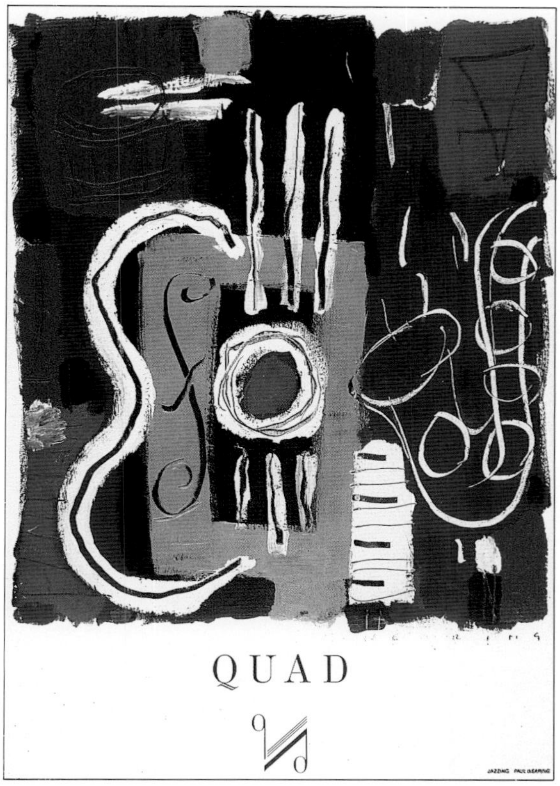

The Quad Hi-Fi Product Range

CLIENT: Quad Electro-acoustics Limited, Huntingdon, Cambridgeshire, UK

DESIGNER: Dinah Lone, RSCG Conran Design, London, UK

ILLUSTRATORS: Paul Wearing, Andrew Hirniak

DATE OF COMPLETION: The last poster was printed in November 1990. This is an on-going project with new posters commissioned when budgets allow

TARGET MARKET: Mainly serious music lovers, also hi-fi enthusiasts

PLACE OF SALE: Independent hi-fi retailers and department stores

CLIENT'S BRIEF: To identify a 'Quad' area primarily within listening rooms. Also for use in window displays and exhibition stands. An inexpensive, high-quality solution which must work within a wide range of standards of interiors and situations and be implemented by the retailer with no guidelines.

DESIGN RATIONALE: A2 format posters with a consistent layout combining the image area and the Quad identity in a set of 'Fine Art' posters. The use of highly creative and diverse imagery directly inspired by different types of music, such as opera, jazz and classical, to appeal to the serious music lover.

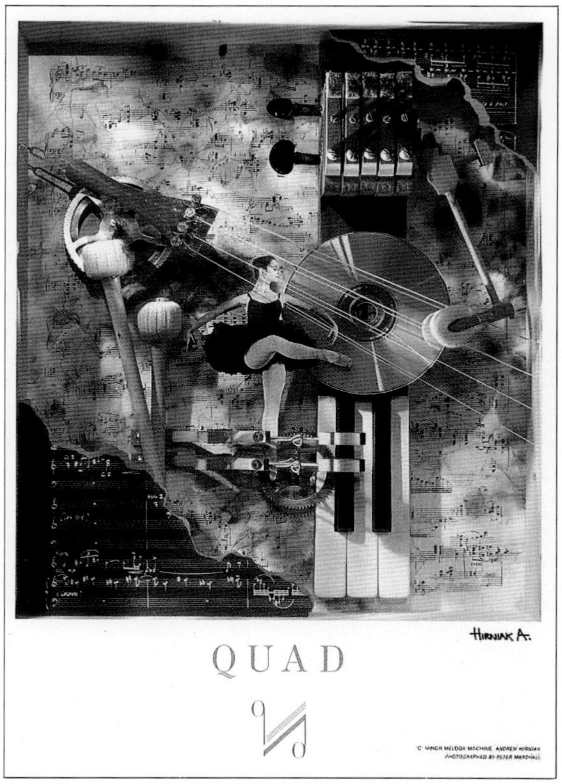

Theme Poster

CLIENT: Thresher Wine Shops, Welwyn Garden City, Herts, UK

DESCRIPTION OF PRODUCT: Theme poster paper/screen printing 30in × 40in

DESIGNER: Hanneka Steenmetz, Nucleus Design, Thames Ditton, Surrey, UK

ILLUSTRATOR: Lawrence Zeegan

DATE OF COMPLETION: January 1991

TARGET MARKET: Thresher customers

PLACE OF SALE: Thresher Wine Stores

CLIENT'S BRIEF: To design a range of point-of-sale material to promote a 'sale' in which shop managers would be able to promote individual products.

DESIGN RATIONALE: The theme 'Wrap Up a Winter Bargain' was developed to communicate the special offer message. This was then interpreted in a bold, graphic and distinctive way, combining informal illustration with striking colours.

Theme Poster

CLIENT: Thresher Wine Shops, Welwyn Garden City, Herts, UK

DESCRIPTION OF PRODUCT: Theme poster paper/screen printing 30in × 40in

DESIGNER: Troy Litten, Nucleus Design, Thames Ditton, Surrey, UK

ILLUSTRATOR: In-house

DATE OF COMPLETION: March 1991

TARGET MARKET: Wine customers

PLACE OF SALE: Thresher Wine Stores

CLIENT'S BRIEF: To create a visual theme to assist in promoting a new range of 40 Southern France wines.

DESIGN RATIONALE: The title 'The Beautiful South' was created to give the promotion a memorable theme. Designs were created that combined an impactful graphic 'icon' with a bold, but appropriate, use of colour.

BHS Fashion Themes

CLIENT: British Home Stores, London, UK

DESIGNER: James Pyott, London, UK

LAUNCH DATE: 1989

PLACE OF SALE: British Home Stores retail outlets

CLIENT'S BRIEF: Point-of sale for in-store promotion of fashion themes. The design had to promote and show off mannequins which stood in front of the banners.

BHS Price Reduction

CLIENT: British Home Stores, London, UK

DESIGNER: James Pyott, London, UK

LAUNCH DATE: 1989

PLACE OF SALE: British Home Stores retail outlets

CLIENT'S BRIEF: To produce a strong and aggressive campaign to announce a reduction in prices owing to refurbishment.

BHS Summer Fashions

CLIENT: British Home Stores, London, UK

DESIGNER: James Pyott, London, UK

LAUNCH DATE: 1989

PLACE OF SALE: British Home Stores retail outlets

CLIENT'S BRIEF: Summer shop was designed to promote summer fashions within the store to generally make the shop feel exciting. Also it had to act as a backdrop to display the clothes.

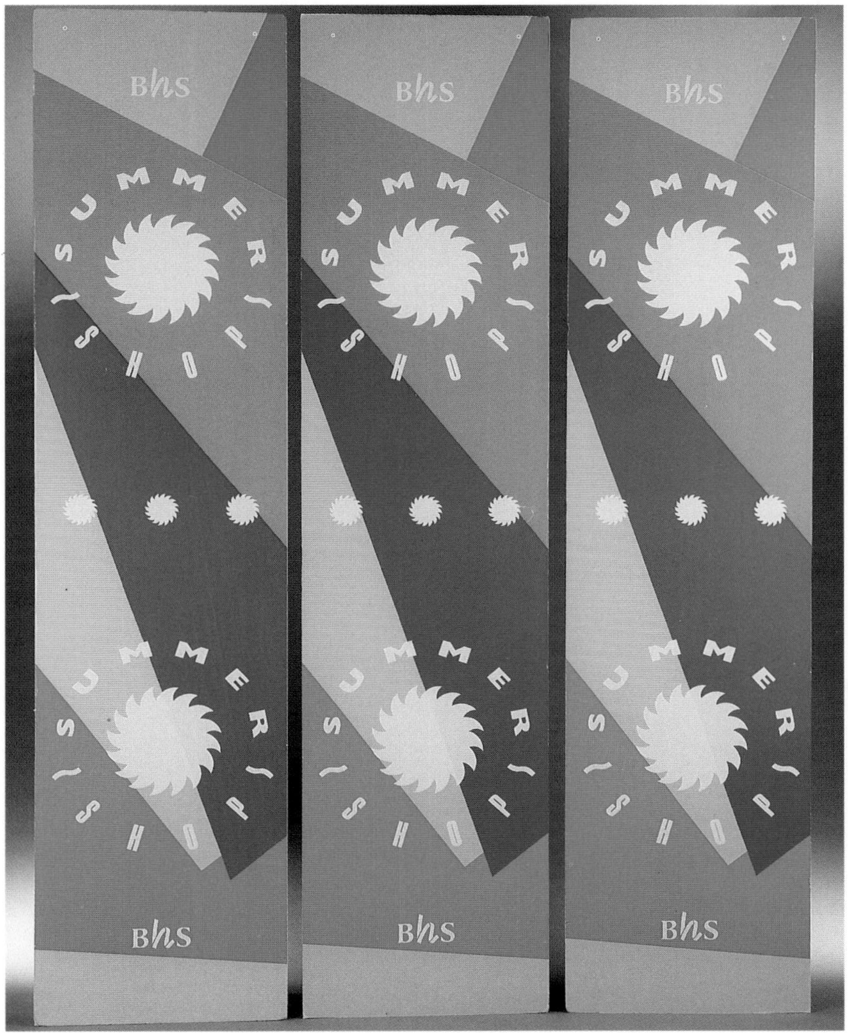

Polaroid Promotion

CLIENT: Polaroid Corporation, London, UK

DESCRIPTION OF PRODUCT: Business and professional packaging, point-of-sale and promotional material

DESIGNER: John Rushworth, Bob Mytton, Pentagram Design Ltd, London, UK

DATE OF COMPLETION: 1989

CLIENT'S BRIEF: Speed, confidentiality and accuracy make Polaroid instant film valuable for business and professional use, and as an effective means of communication. New packaging, point-of-sale and promotional material was designed to promote this aspect of Polaroid.

Alain Mikli Glasses

CLIENT: Alain Mikli, Paris, France

DESCRIPTION OF PRODUCT: Wood silhouette display stand

DESIGNER: Pat PLV, Puteaux, France

DATE OF COMPLETION: 1987

PLACE OF SALE: Opticians

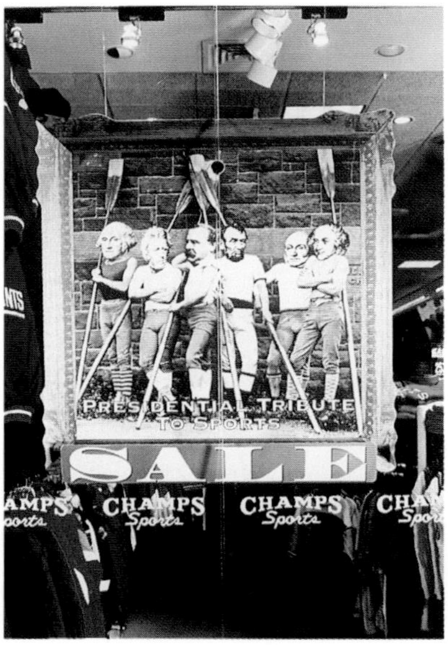
PRESIDENTIAL TRIBUTE
TO SPORTS
SALE
CHAMPS
Sports

SPRING TIME SAL

NBA BIG SHOTS
SPALDING
NBA
PISTONS
11

Athletics Equipment

CLIENT: Champs Sports, New York, USA

DESCRIPTION OF PRODUCT: 18pt board for mannequin heads

DESIGNER: Medallion Associates, New York, USA

DATE OF COMPLETION: February 1992

TARGET MARKET: Primarily males aged 13–19, but also males aged 19–26

PLACE OF SALE: Champs Sports (athletic footwear, apparel and equipment retailer)

CLIENT'S BRIEF: To design a window display that would promote a specific theme.

FOUR CORNERS
FOUR CORNERS

AMSTERDAM
CITY
MILAN
Rome
NEW YORK
Breaks
PARIS

Four Corners

CLIENT: Leagus Delaney, London, UK

DESCRIPTION OF PRODUCT: Silk screen panels

DESIGNER: The Partners, London, UK

ILLUSTRATOR OR PHOTOGRAPHER: 'British Breaks' Panel: Geoffrey Appleton; 'Great Trains' Panel: Line + Line; 'Planes' Panel: Malcolm English

DATE OF COMPLETION: April 1989

TARGET MARKET: Retail

PLACE OF SALE: Four Corners travel agents – window display

CLIENT'S BRIEF: To get over to the public that Four Corners was a travel agent; rotographic panels were to be used as part of different promotions within the store.

DESIGN RATIONALE: The design was constrained by having to use existing rotographic panels. It was decided to concentrate on the word of the theme and to make the word as lively, large and visually exciting as possible to draw people into the shop.

DE GROOT COLL
10
15
20
30
40
50
130 FT OF FRONTAGE
YOND MEASURE
CORNER

Signage to Advertise Retail Space

CLIENT: SC Properties, London, UK

DESIGNER: The Partners, London, UK

ILLUSTRATOR OR PHOTOGRAPHER: Mathew Weinreb

SIGN MANUFACTURE: Jon Goodwin

DATE OF COMPLETION: November/December 1991

TARGET MARKET: International retailers

PLACE OF SALE: Corner building of Piccadilly and Old Bond Street – shop window

CLIENT'S BRIEF: A window display for the large retail site on the corner of Piccadilly and Old Bond Street, which would attract international retailers.

DESIGN RATIONALE: The display takes the form of a giant surveyor's tape running the entire length of the shop front (approximately 45m/140ft).

Store Promotion – Christmas

CLIENT: Paperchase, London, UK

DESCRIPTION OF PRODUCT: From small tree decorations on card to 7′ × 3′ window displays on board

DESIGNER: Janine Hall/Chris Keeble, Keeble & Hall, London, UK

ILLUSTRATOR: Boy & Horse: Graham Philpot; Special lettering: Alan Dempsey

DATE OF COMPLETION: Autumn 1989

TARGET MARKET: Christmas shoppers

PLACE OF SALE: Paperchase: specialist paper and giftstores

CLIENT'S BRIEF: To create a traditional warm Victorian Christmas theme capable of working on carrier bags, point-of-sale window displays, product packaging, in-store siting.

DESIGN RATIONALE: To take the client's brief and translate it into graphics – the central element is redrawn from an old Victorian engraving of a boy on a rocking horse (which is now produced in colour) which is supported by special hand-drawn lettering and a green colour theme

Christmas Novelties and Soft Toys
Useful Notepads and Files for Office Home or School.
Seasonal Gift Tags and Stickers for special Messages
Gift Boxes Tapes and Ribbons
Writing Papers and envelopes in all Colours
Fine Christmas Tinsel of all Kinds and Colours
Happy Christmas and New Year
Pens and pencils for every stocking.
Wrapping Papers for Every Present
Unusual Tree Decorations Baubles and Garlands
Christmas Crackers in Various Sizes & Colours
Christmas Novelties and Soft Toys
Special Christmas Cards for Family & Friends.
Paper Plates & Napkins for Parties
Gift Boxes Tapes and Ribbons
Magical Christmas decorations Streamers & Poppers
Smart Diaries and Address Books
Useful Notepads and Files for Office Home or School.
Writing Papers and envelopes in all Colours
Pens and pencils for every stocking.
Wrapping Papers for Every Present
Seasonal Gift Tags and Stickers for special Messages
From all our Stores
Smart Diaries and Address Books
From all our Stores

Hanging cards (above) and carrier bags (opposite) – part of the Paperchase Christmas display material designed by Keeble and Hall. See also pp 48–9.

SOMETHING SPECIAL FROM PAPERCHASE AT CHRISTMAS
PAPERCHASE
AT · CHRISTMAS
HAPPY CHRISTMAS and NEW YEAR
Writing papers and envelopes ~in~ all Colours
Pens and pencils for every stocking
Unusual Tree Decorations Baubles and Garlands
Christmas Crackers in Various Sizes & Colours
Paper Plates & Napkins for Parties
Magical Christmas decorations
Fine Christmas Tinsel all kinds and Colours
Wrapping Papers for every present
Christmas Novelties and Soft Toys
Special Christmas Cards for Family & Friends
Gift Boxes Tapes and Ribbons
Smart Diaries and Address Books
From all our Stores
Seasonal Gift Tags and Stickers for special

CORAL
"PENALTY INSIDE THE 22...
...AN EASY KICK TO WIN THE MATCH...
...OH NO, I DON'T BELIEVE IT"
WHO'LL BE OVERJOYED AT THE FINAL WHISTLE?

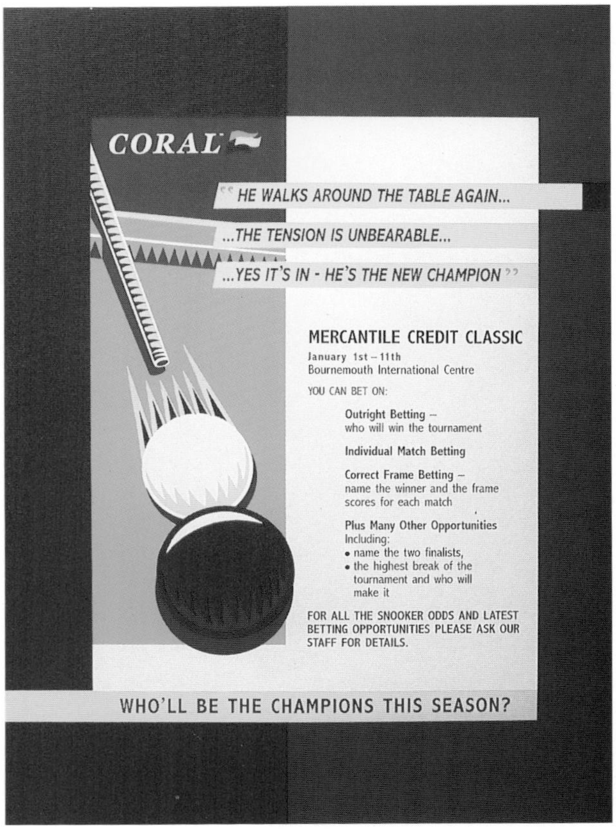
CORAL
"HE WALKS AROUND THE TABLE AGAIN...
...THE TENSION IS UNBEARABLE...
...YES IT'S IN - HE'S THE NEW CHAMPION"
MERCANTILE CREDIT CLASSIC
January 1st – 11th
Bournemouth International Centre
YOU CAN BET ON:
Outright Betting – who will win the tournament
Individual Match Betting
Correct Frame Betting – name the winner and the frame scores for each match
Plus Many Other Opportunities Including:
• name the two finalists,
• the highest break of the tournament and who will make it
FOR ALL THE SNOOKER ODDS AND LATEST BETTING OPPORTUNITIES PLEASE ASK OUR STAFF FOR DETAILS.
WHO'LL BE THE CHAMPIONS THIS SEASON?

HORSES
HORSES

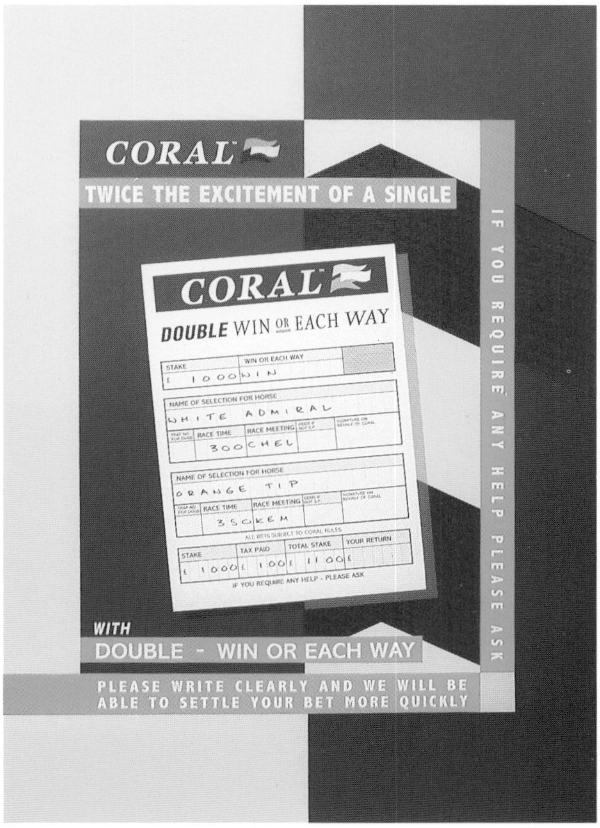

Coral Betting Shop

CLIENT: Coral, Barking, Essex, UK

DESCRIPTION OF PRODUCT: Window graphics to promote betting shops

DESIGNER: Brem Bremner & Russ O'Donnell, Light & Coley Ltd, London, UK

ILLUSTRATOR OR PHOTOGRAPHER: Chris Dreja

DATE OF COMPLETION: Spring 1992

TARGET MARKET: Existing and potential new consumers

PLACE OF SALE: Betting shop services on the high street

CLIENT'S BRIEF: To develop point-of-sale for the betting shop windows that would create excitement and appeal to both existing and potential customers. The images could not be accompanied with any words and had to break the mould of traditional, clichéd horse racing imagery.

DESIGN RATIONALE: Light & Coley developed images that both pulled the observer into the action and conversely projected the action into the high street. The designs communicated sporting excitement in the broadest sense and endorsed the overall Coral plan of broadening the appeal of the betting shop both in terms of the product on offer and to a wider audience.

CORA
reusch
reusch
reusch
reusch
CORA

L ™
COAL
9
21

LONELY HEARTS
MINI HIFI
● HANDSOME ORIENTAL, single, attractive, sincere, intelligent, caring, seeks similar with somewhere to take me home to, to share the good things.
Box No. FH 1215CD
▶ Programmable Compact Disc Player with shuffle play
▶ 45 watts RMS per channel amplifier with 7-band graphic equaliser
▶ FM Stereo/LW/MW quartz lock digital synthesised tuner with 20 random pre-sets
▶ Auto-reverse cassette deck with Dolby 'B' noise reduction*
▶ Remote control
▶ APM speakers
SONY
THE POWER OF SOUND
SONY
SONY

LONELY HEARTS
MINI HIFI
● Mr FILOFAX where are you? Music lover (unused!) non-scene, seeks introduction to cosmopolitan lifestyle. Solvent, clean cut, enjoys occasional cuddles.
Box No. FH 1205CD
▶ Programmable Compact Disc Player with shuffle play
▶ 25 watts RMS per channel amplifier with 3-band graphic equaliser
▶ FM Stereo/LW/MW tuner
▶ Dynamic optimum loudness function
▶ Double cassette deck with Dolby 'B' noise reduction* and continuous play
▶ APM speakers
SONY
THE POWER OF SOUND
SONY
SONY
YEAR PLANNER

Sony Mini Hi-Fi System

CLIENT: Sony UK Ltd, Staines, Middlesex, UK

DESCRIPTION OF PRODUCT: Three-piece portable mini hi-fi system (upright) 225 × 370 × 275mm; speakers (each) 185 × 115 × 225mm

DESIGNER: Martin Smith, Clarke Hooper Consulting, Slough, Berkshire, UK

ILLUSTRATOR OR PHOTOGRAPHER: Andy Holmes

DATE OF COMPLETION: 1988

TARGET MARKET: Under-35s: affluent and mobile

PLACE OF SALE: Sony centres, independent Sony stockists and high street electrical multiples.

CLIENT'S BRIEF: The Sony new mini hi-fi system was the first hi-fi system to offer consumers true 'portability'. The brief from Sony was to produce innovative, eye-catching generic point-of-sale aimed at the younger, affluent, 80s 'yuppie' market.

DESIGN RATIONALE: Some humour was needed to differentiate Sony black boxes, together with a very stylized graphic approach that would appeal to the target market and ensure the product and point-of-sale stood out in-store. Hence, the link with *Time Out* magazine and the publication's 'Lonely Hearts' columns.

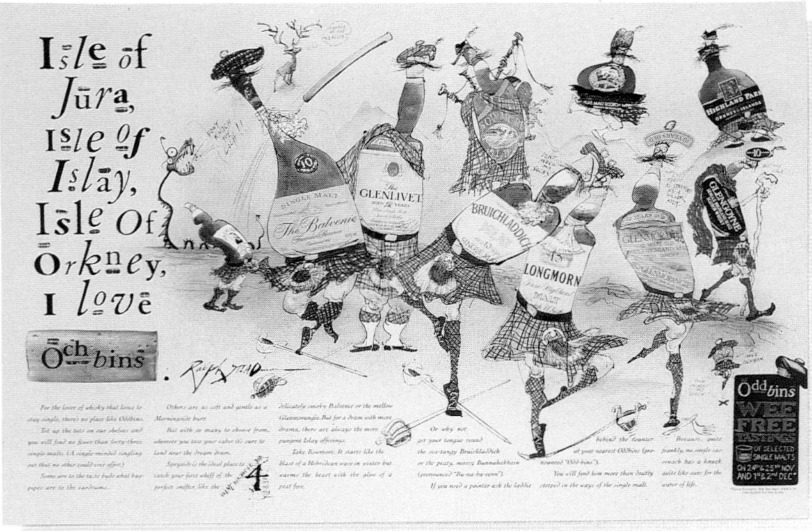

Oddbins Posters

CLIENT: Oddbins, London, UK

DESIGNER: Miller & Leeves, London, UK

Spanish porter: Retail Advertising Services, London, UK

ILLUSTRATOR: Ralph Steadman

DATE OF COMPLETION: 1989–1992

TARGET MARKET: Wine drinkers of all ages

PLACE OF SALE: Off licences

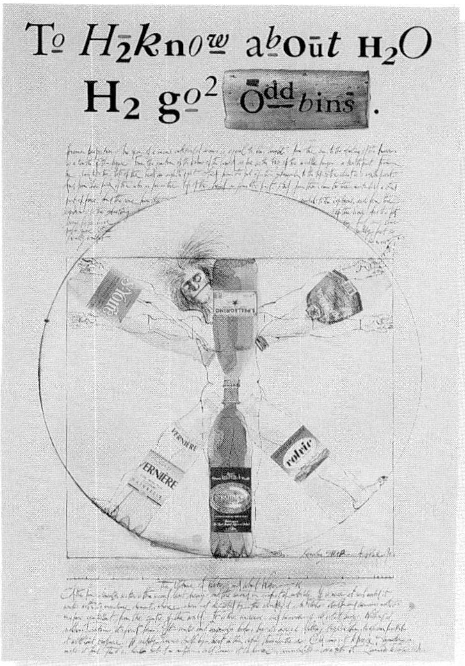
To H_2know about H_2O
H_2 go^2 Oddbins.

Quantitas.
Qualitas.
Quaffumfast.
(Get a firm grasp
of the classics at Oddbins.)

Spain
WINES FROM SPAIN

Floor-standing units Most supermarket chains and large-scale retail outlets have their share of floor-standing merchanizers, dump bins, "gondolas" and dispensers. They are often situated at the end of an aisle or a run of units, and manufacturers launching a new product or brand – coordinated with a burst of advertising – will negotiate (and often pay for) space to put in their own construction. These have the advantage of isolating the product from its competitors, and displaying, in a controlled environment, a larger quantity of the product than might otherwise be possible.

Some products, like sunglasses, look much better when displayed on specially designed fittings that retailers cannot provide or do not have shelf space for. Some products, like cars, are often sold in spaces where no display facilities or wall fittings are provided. Some products, like tapes and CDs, sell better when demonstration facilities are provided. And when these facilities, these units, these fittings, look attractive, stylish and well-designed, the products move that much quicker.

HERE.
GR-A1
GR-S707
JOIN
A UNIQUE
CLUB
SSORIES SUPPLIED WITH
JVC VIDEO CAMERAS
JVC
PRODUCT TRAINING
Adaptor/Battery Charger

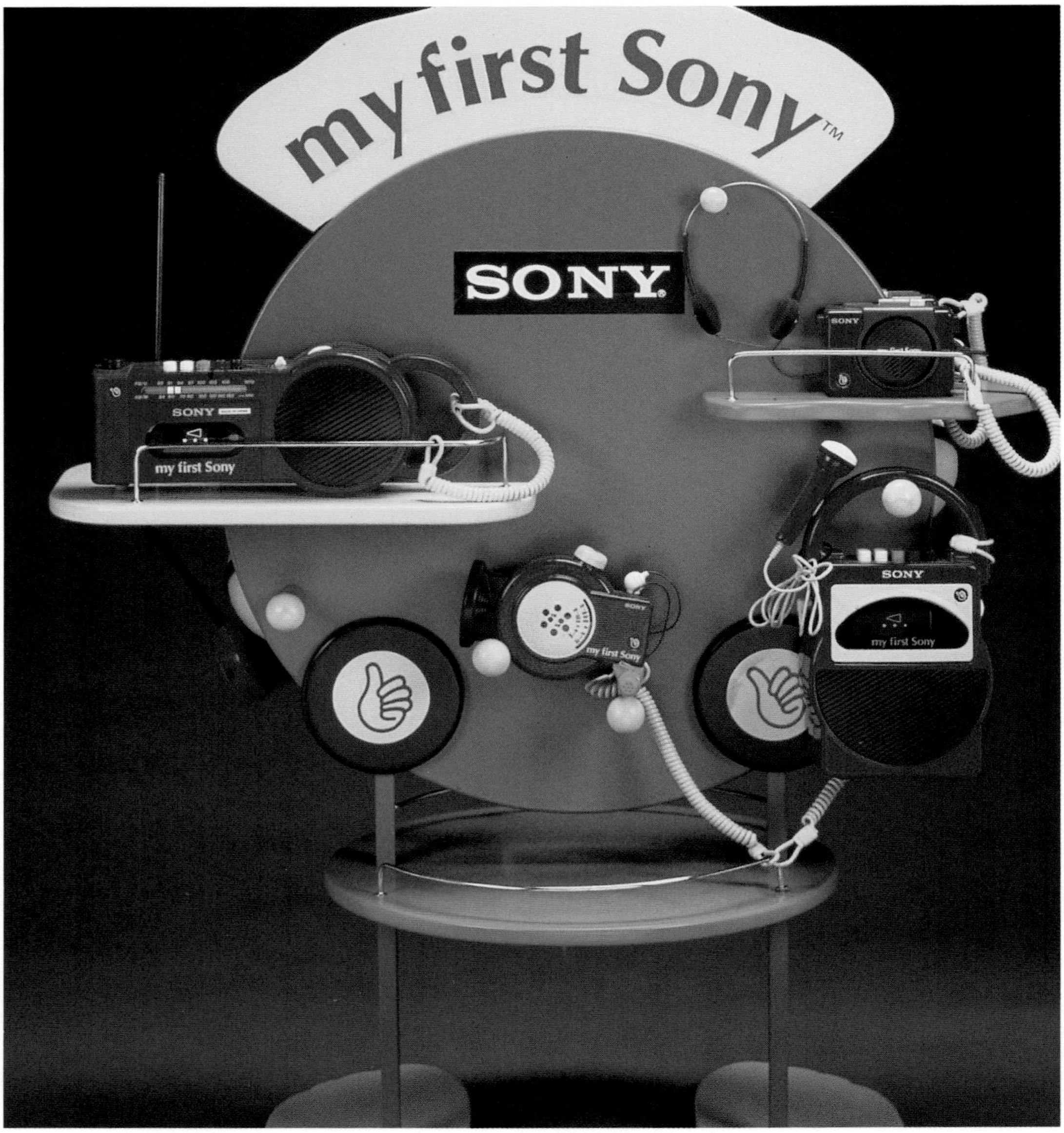

My First Sony Floor-Standing Merchandizer

CLIENT: Sony UK Ltd, Staines, Middlesex, UK

DESCRIPTION OF PRODUCT: Floor-standing merchandizer. Size: Height 1260mm, Width 910mm, Depth 580mm. Materials: medium-density fibreboard, spray-finish non-toxic paint, screen-printed graphics. Supplied as flat pack – retailer to construct

DESIGNER: Alan Taylor, Creative Director, Oakley Young 4th Dimension, Leicester, UK

DATE OF COMPLETION: 1991–1992 (on-going)

TARGET MARKET: Male and female (age 3–10 years) and adult interest

PLACE OF SALE: Sony Centres UK, Sony Europe: Switzerland/Denmark. Also UK independent electrical retail outlets

CLIENT'S BRIEF: To increase awareness and therefore sales of the My First Sony range. To convey an image of quality, unique features, ease of use and safety, targeting the younger persons introduction to audio products.

DESIGN RATIONALE: The My First Sony bar was designed to appeal not only to children but to adults, with all products easily demonstrable to both through a bright and attractive fun-packed floor merchandizer. Height and scale were of major importance. The unit has no sharp edges and is strong and stable. Security is maintained through coloured cables which form part of the display.

My First Sony

CLIENT: Sony France, Paris, France

DESCRIPTION OF PRODUCT: Cardboard and sheet metal; size: height 2000mm; width 800mm; depth 800mm

DESIGNER: Prisme, Suresnes, France

DATE OF COMPLETION: June 1991

TARGET MARKET: Children

PLACE OF SALE: Sony's traditional point-of-sale and toy shops.

CLIENT'S BRIEF: To create a permanent floor display to demonstrate the 17 products of the My First Sony line targeted for four- to ten-year-olds. The 17 products must be able to be used but not carried off. It also had to reflect that Sony's high technology and quality standards are not only for grown ups but also for children.

DESIGN RATIONALE: To answer these requirements the designers chose a square tower that a child could have built himself with sand or Lego. It was given the Sony look by using black lacquered sheet metal. The black matte background also emphasizes the bright colours of the products, the roof recalls these colours. The products are mounted on the side of the tower, the level of each product depending on the age of the user.

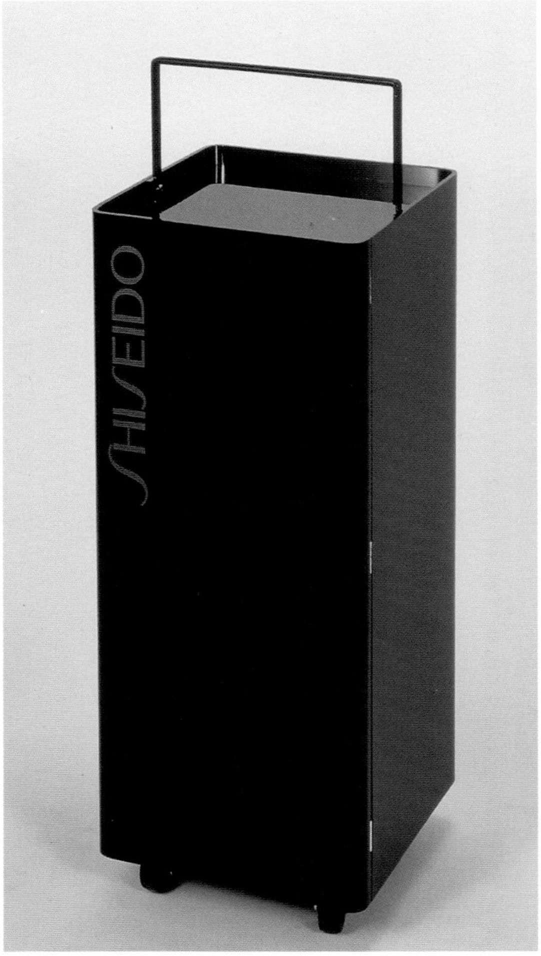

Window Support for Make-up

CLIENT: Shiseido, Paris, France

DESCRIPTION OF PRODUCT: Cardboard and black Plexi

DESIGNER: Jean-Pierre Toth, Méthacryl, Paris, France

DATE OF COMPLETION: 1990

PLACE OF SALE: Department stores and perfumeries

CLIENT'S BRIEF: To respect the Shiseido identity and colour code (black and red); to use geometrical shapes.

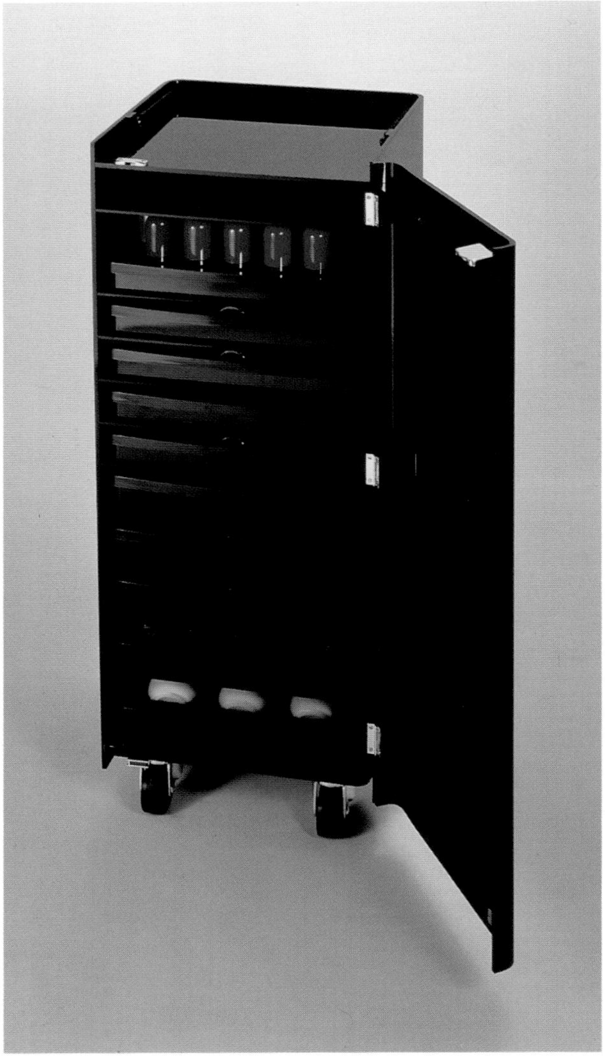

Battistoni Cigarettes

CLIENT: Philip Morris Europe SA, Lausanne, Switzerland

DESCRIPTION OF PRODUCT: Plexiglas; size 60 × 60 × 200cm

DESIGNER: Maurice Progin, Lausanne, Switzerland

ILLUSTRATOR OR PHOTOGRAPHER: Horst Neuffer, Lausanne, Switzerland

DATE OF COMPLETION: 1990

TARGET MARKET: Duty free customers

PLACE OF SALE: Tax-free world exhibition for launching new product

CLIENT'S BRIEF: To make something attractive in accordance with the marketing information and brand image.

Camcorder Demonstration Unit

CLIENT: JVC., London, UK

DESCRIPTION OF UNIT: Laminated MDF construction using electronic switching gear

DESIGNER: Paul Osborne, Buchanan Group, London, UK

DATE OF COMPLETION: 1991

TARGET MARKET: 25–50 age group

PLACE OF SALE: Brown goods retail outlets

CLIENT'S BRIEF: To demonstrate JVC's range of camcorders

DESIGN RATIONALE: To design a compact, secure unit that could demonstrate camcorders by using an electronic comparitor unit, and also display accessories.

Camcorder Bar

CLIENT: Sharp Electronics, London, UK

DESCRIPTION OF PRODUCT: Metal laminated MDF construction using electronic switching equipment

DESIGNER: Paul Osborne, Buchanan Group, London, UK

DATE OF COMPLETION: 1990

TARGET MARKET: 25–50 age group

PLACE OF SALE: Brown goods retail outlets

CLIENT'S BRIEF: To design a camcorder unit to display a range of camcorders.

DESIGN RATIONALE: A compact camcorder unit that allows a "hands on", secure demonstration unit to give the customer the opportunity to use and compare the camcorders using an electronics switching system.

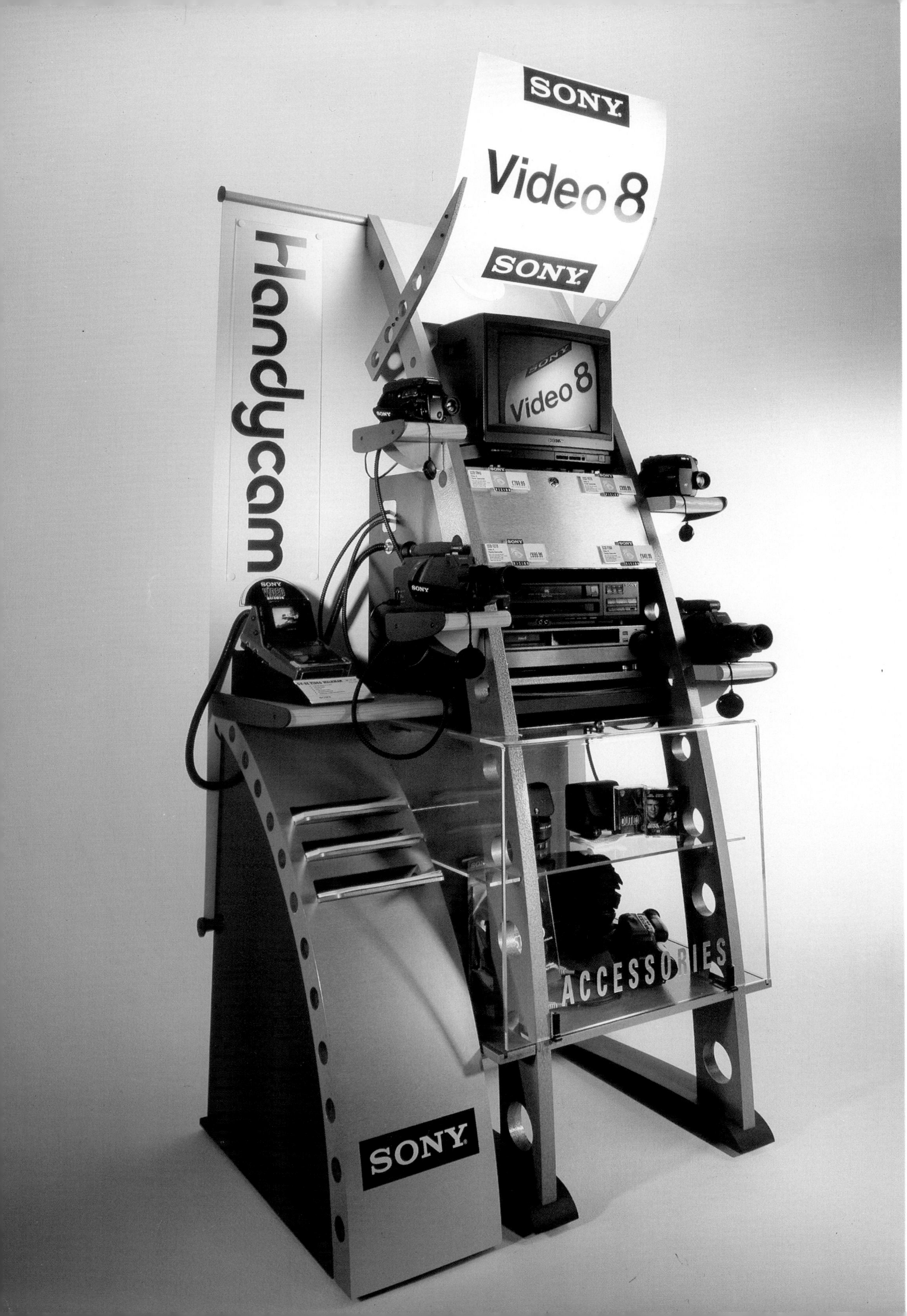

SONY
Video 8
SONY
Handycam
Video 8
ACCESSORIES
SONY

Sony Video Camcorder

CLIENT: Sony UK Ltd, Staines, Middlesex, UK
DESCRIPTION OF PRODUCT: Floor-standing Video 8 Interactive Comparitor, demonstrating four Sony camcorders with full home studio edit facility, also demonstrating Video 8 Walkman/Promotional VCR to main monitor. Electronic control system also securitized the products by alarm with non-mains battery back-up. Lockable accessories display cabinet for software. Size: Height 2030mm, Width 1m, Depth 700mm
DESIGNER: Mr Alan Taylor, Creative Director, Oakley Young 4th Dimension, Leicester, UK
PHOTOGRAPHER: Barry Goodwin
DATE OF COMPLETION: 1991–1992 (on-going)
TARGET MARKET: 18-plus
PLACE OF SALE: Sony Centres UK. Also UK independent electrical retail outlets (approximately 800 in total)
CLIENT'S BRIEF: To increase Sony's 'in-store' share of camcorder sales at selected independent dealers; to develop product turn of camcorders at store levels through effective hands-on; to obtain additional spaces for Sony apart from current camcorder bars.
DESIGN RATIONALE: The unit is designed to allow the customer to pick up the camcorders and try them – a vital element in achieving consumer acceptance in the rapidly changing camcorder market. The bar displays the complete range of Video 8 products and accessories, and enables the consumer to compare relevant features.

Motorola

CLIENT: Motorola, Netherlands
DESCRIPTION OF PRODUCT: Display Unit for Motorola telephones
DESIGNER: Alrec POS Design, Hillegorn, The Netherlands

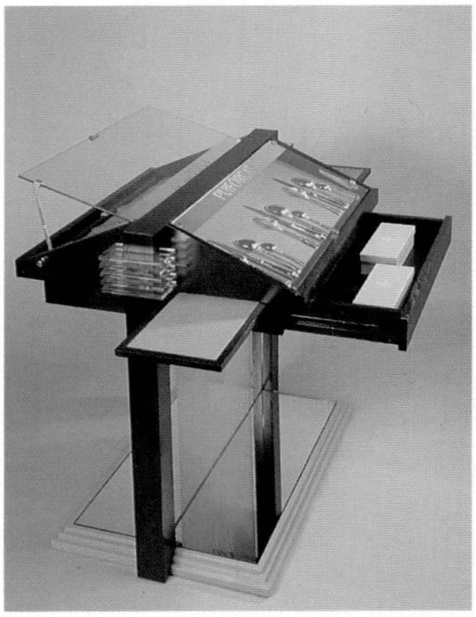

Puiforcat

CLIENT: Puiforcat, La Plaine Saint Denis, France

DESCRIPTION OF PRODUCT: Wood, glass and steel. Size: width 1100mm; height 1060mm; depth 750mm.

DESIGNER: Prisme, Suresnes, France

DATE OF COMPLETION: September 1990

TARGET MARKET: Higher class market

PLACE OF SALE: Retail

CLIENT'S BRIEF: Recently Puiforcat has become established in new points-of-sale other than its own shops. This cabinet has been designed to convey the quality and the aesthetism of the make.

DESIGN RATIONALE: To respect the styles created by Jean Puiforcat the cabinet was given a '1930 type look'. The identification of the Puiforcat brand mark is provided firstly by the luminous Puiforcat logo on the drop leaves of the presentation tables and, secondly, by the design of the goblet which is a key element of the Puiforcat make. More subtly, the five fins of luminous glass on either side of the cabinet repeat an important decorative element of the stone frontage of the new Puiforcat boutique in Avenue Matignon, Paris.

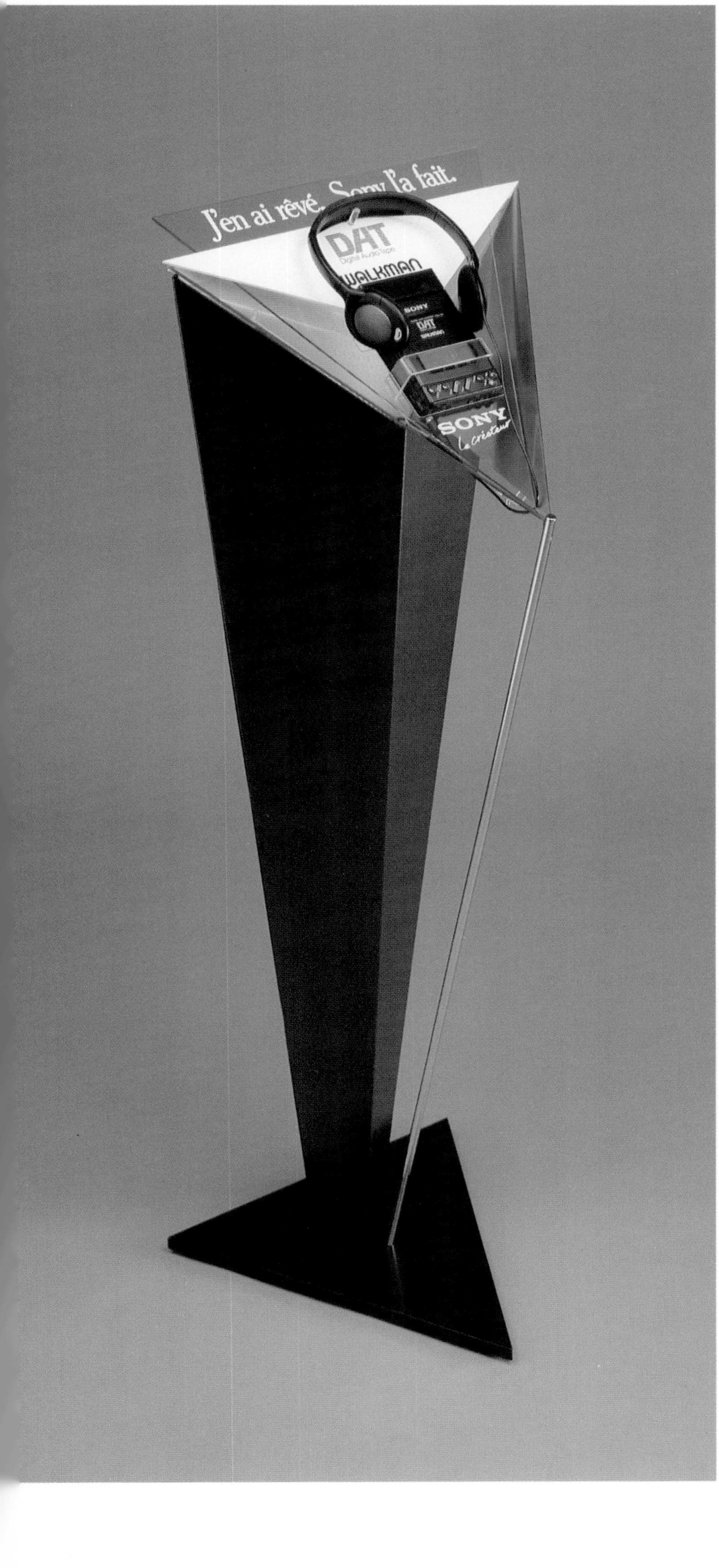

Sony Dat Walkman

CLIENT: Sony France, Paris, France

DESCRIPTION OF PRODUCT: Laminated wood and lacquered sheet metal, acrylic vacuum-forming electric equipment. Size: height 1200mm; width 380mm; depth 420mm.

DESIGNER: Prisme, Suresnes, France

DATE OF COMPLETION: April 1991

PLACE OF SALE: Specialist hi-fi video stores

CLIENT'S BRIEF: To enhance the latest Sony creation: the digital audio tape Walkman, a unique product owing to its innovative and its highly technical nature in the market. To translate the technical nature of the product into the visual impact of the display stand, and to encourage the consumer to try the product on the spot.

DESIGN RATIONALE: To embody the idea of high technology, the stand incorporates the feeling of a sleek simple work of modern art. A sharp line in the design was chosen to emphasize the ultimate in technical advances. The Walkman is illuminated from below to evoke the light of genius and science. The Walkman is firmly attached to the stand while making it easy for the consumer to try it out.

Honda Freestanding Display

CLIENT: Honda UK, London, UK

DESCRIPTION OF PRODUCT: Laminated MDF structure incorporating custom-designed LV lighting and cable system

DESIGNER: Paul Osborne, Buchanan Group, London, UK

DATE OF COMPLETION: 1990

TARGET MARKET: 30–50 age group

PLACE OF SALE: Honda dealerships

CLIENT'S BRIEF: To enhance the Honda environment and inject continuity into their dealerships nationwide.

DESIGN rationale: To use a classic column approach using LV lighting and lightboxes on a cable system to further promote the Honda range and serve to both enhance and punctuate the dealership environment.

HONDA
approved cars

Jacques Dessange Make-up Stand

CLIENT: Jacques Dessange, Paris, France

DESCRIPTION OF PRODUCT: Presentation display piece for a range of make-up

DESIGNER: Jean-Réné Guegan, Ekonos, Paris, France

DATE OF COMPLETION: November 1989

TARGET MARKET: Clients of the Jacques Dessange hairdressing salons, and certain pharmacies

CLIENT'S BRIEF: To research and conceive a presentation display piece for an entire range of make up; it had to be coherent with the graphic image developed for the range of make-up.

DESIGN RATIONALE: The presentation of the whole range reflected the nuances of each range of products: face make-up, powder, lipstick, nail polish and mascara.

Display for Solars of Stendhal

CLIENT: Sanofi Beauté, Paris, France

DESCRIPTION OF PRODUCT: This display is composed of garden furniture, including an armchair, a footstool and a tea trolley. All these elements piled up form the basic structure of the display. Backing form boxes carry the products. Dimensions: 180 × 40 × 40cm.

DESIGNER: RS Creation, Montreuil, France

DATE OF COMPLETION: 1987

TARGET MARKET: Top-end market

PLACE OF SALE: Specialized perfume shops and retailers

CLIENT'S BRIEF: To create a display table to stock sun-care products on rollers, easy to use and taking up little space, that reminded customers of the sun, and that the retailer could use afterwards.

DESIGN RATIONALE: The theme used is both playful and functional, the yellow canvas being reminiscent of sunshine. The re-usable aspect of the elements is an important factor for the retailer. A counter display was also distributed.

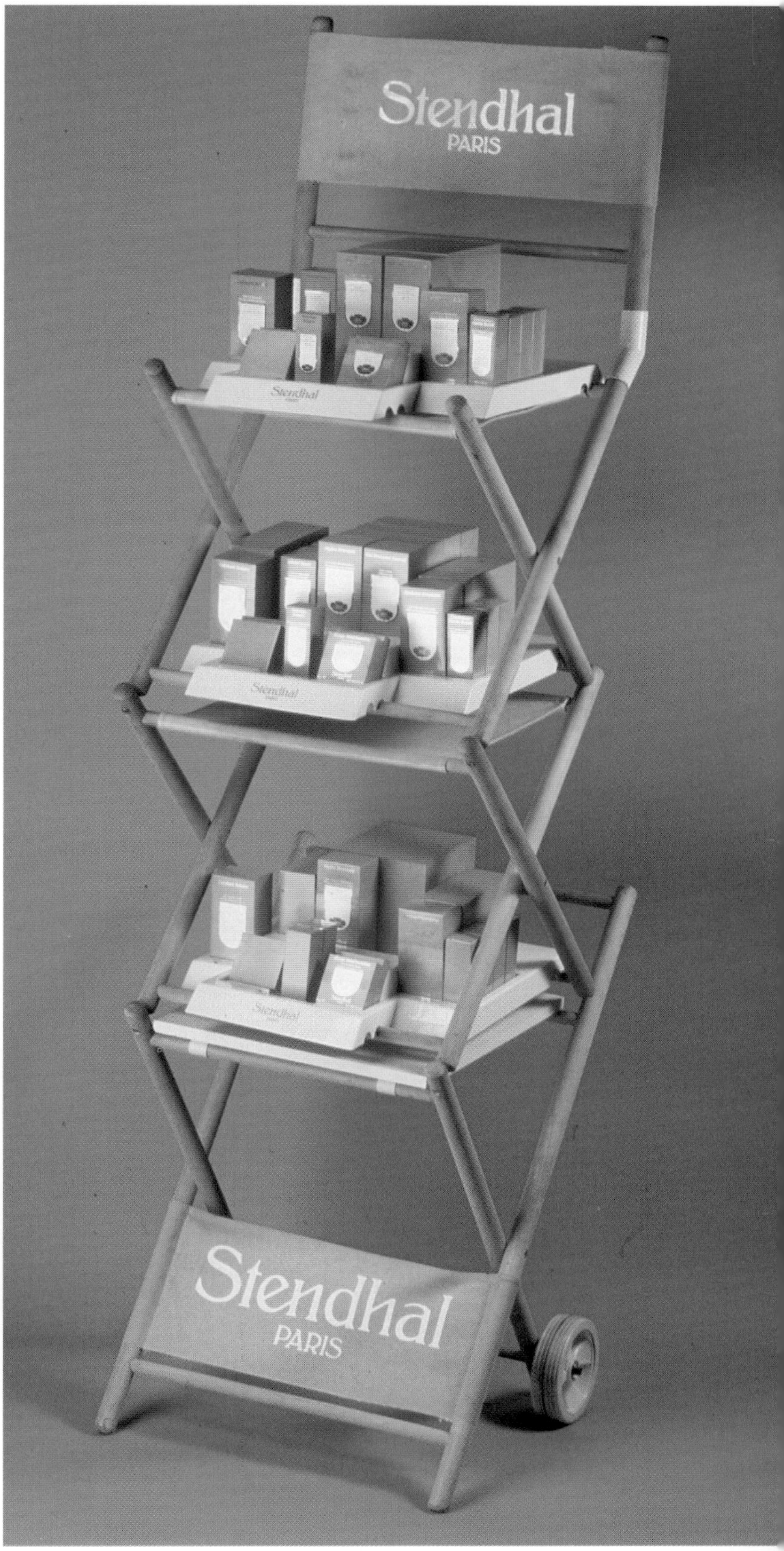

Miele 'Black Diamond'

CLIENT: Miele France, Paris, France

DESCRIPTION OF PRODUCT: Vacuum cleaner

DESIGNER: Ateliers Reunis, Bagnolet, France

DATE OF COMPLETION: Summer 1990

TARGET MARKET: Most clients

PLACE OF SALE: Electrical goods retailers: 'Boulanger' group

CLIENT'S BRIEF: Miele France wanted a point-of-sale display which characterized the anthracite grey metallic nature of the vacuum cleaner casing, as well as its compactness.

DESIGN RATIONALE: The idea was to create a display unit which was reminiscent of a wrapped present. The polystyrene mirror in the display showed, in five different angles, the image of the vacuum cleaner like the facets of a diamond – a reminder of its name – 'Black Diamond'. The coldness of the metal and the mirror were 'warmed' by the use of halogen lighting to catch the eye of customers.

Sarah Coventry Sunglasses

CLIENT: R. N. Koch, New York, USA

DESCRIPTION OF PRODUCT: Non-prescription fashion-frame sunglasses for females

DESIGNER: Barry David Berger & Associates, Inc, New York, USA

TARGET MARKET: Mid-level female market

PLACE OF SALE: Mid-level retailers

CLIENT'S BRIEF: To incorporate the following features: 160-frame capacity rotating fixture; modular construction for other potential quantities; high-style fixture to enhance frame style; flexible frame support location; group frames around three to four colour styles

DESIGN RATIONALE: The product layout insured against the homogeneous appearance of the product by orienting the frames in eight directions – four on a bridge support with 'temples' open, four on trays with 'temples' closed; the architectural appearance and neutral background colour enhanced the product styles and amplified the product colour palettes.

Travelling Exhibition of Paloma Picasso

CLIENT: Prestige et Collections Internationale, Paris, France

DESCRIPTION OF PRODUCT: Safety glass and lacquered wood

DESIGNER: Prisme, Suresnes, France

DATE OF COMPLETION: June 1991

TARGET MARKET: Fashion-conscious and top end of the range purchasers – female

PLACE OF SALE: Department stores and European perfumeries

CLIENT'S BRIEF: To design a travelling exhibition stand that can be used in a space ranging from 5 to 20sq m in order to present the world of Paloma Picasso in different countries (Europe, USA, South America). The exhibition had to express Paloma Picasso's personality, not only through her perfume, make-up and bath lines, but also through her other creations: jewellery, leather goods, glasses, china.

DESIGN RATIONALE: Paloma Picasso's personality and image are very strong, her face and her colour have circled the globe. Her theatrical side is also a very important part of her image. A red curtain was the natural source of inspiration for the concept of this exhibit which links entertainment and identity. In order to show the objects and photos to their fullest advantage, three types of exhibition units were created using the same theme.

Paloma Picasso
Paloma Picasso

Image Wall

CLIENT: Porsche Cars Great Britain Ltd, Reading, Berks, UK

DESCRIPTION OF PRODUCT: A series of 2m high modular panels manufactured from heat-formed foamex which can be configured in various combinations to form point-of-sale displays.

DESIGNER: John Furneaux, Furneaux Stewart Design & Communication, London, UK

PHOTOGRAPHER: Nicholas Gentilli

DATE OF COMPLETION: 1989

TARGET MARKET: Official Porsche Centre customers

PLACE OF SALE: Official Porsche Centre Network (dealership network) in Great Britain and worldwide

DESIGN RATIONALE: The brief called for a semi-permanent yet inherently flexible design solution. The system needed to be sufficiently permanent to ensure that the client's products, services and corporate identity were correctly and consistently displayed, yet flexible enough to perform as space divider or pure point-of sale system whenever required.

Weiss Art Products Unit

CLIENT: Weiss Art, Sydney, Australia

DESCRIPTION OF PRODUCT: Extruded aluminium sections; vacuum-formed panels; timber shelving; 1m × 1m × 1m modules

DESIGNER: Design Field Pty Ltd, Paddington, NSW, Australia

PHOTOGRAPHER: Rob Little, Sydney, Australia

TARGET MARKET: Department stores and tourist retail outlets

CLIENT'S BRIEF: To design and prototype a point-of-sale display for the exclusive range of Weiss fashion products, which include such diverse items as T-shirts, umbrellas, knitting kits, beach towels, sneakers and sweatshirts. Added to this was the requirement that the products could be sold in any number of countries.

DESIGN RATIONALE: The solution was a pack-flat, flexible display system, which, to avoid language and communication problems, used symbols to show the product and pattern, complementing the bold graphic style of the Weiss Art products themselves. The strong visual form of the structure allowed a wide range of products to be displayed homogeneously.

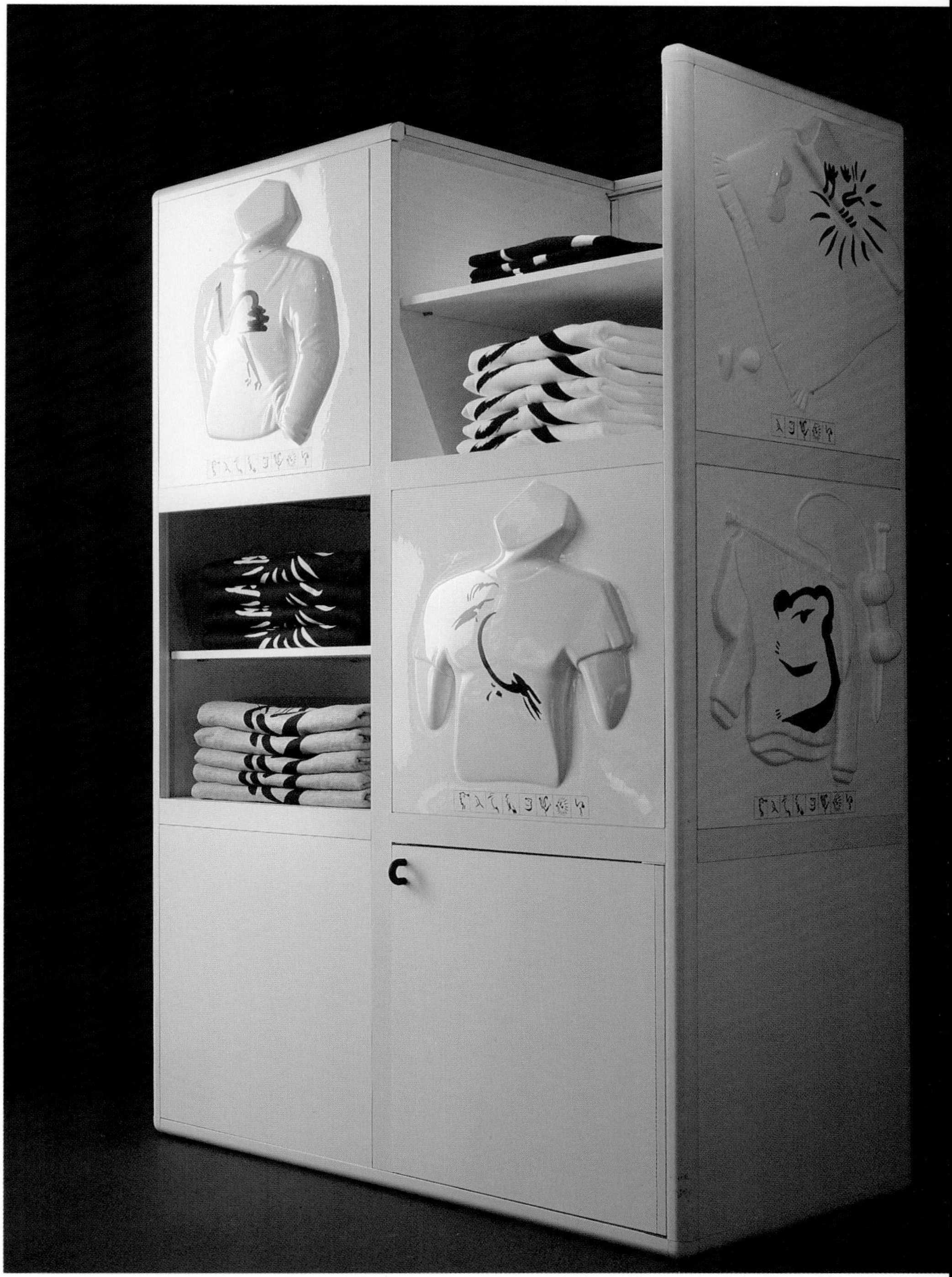

L'espace Valrhona

CLIENT: Valrhona, Tain l'Hermitage, France

DESCRIPTION OF PRODUCT: Metal display stand presenting the whole range of Valrhona products. Height: 2m; width: 30cm

DESIGNER: MBD Design, Bagnolet Cedex, France

DATE OF COMPLETION: February 1992

TARGET MARKET: Baker's shops

CLIENT'S BRIEF: The stand display had to reinforce the brand and product image in baker's shops. The design work had to take into consideration the problem of space. Generally the retail outlets are very small.

DESIGN RATIONALE: MBD Design wanted to keep a strong image in line with the logo and the products. The proposition for the stand display was a square totem, presenting, keeping and distributing the whole range of Valrhona products.

The square can be found on the brand image and the "carrés" of Caraibes et Guanala. The impact comes from the height of the display stand although the constraint on the space is respected with its limited width.

Listening Stand

CLIENT: Virgin Retail Ltd, London, UK

DESIGNER: 20/20 Design & Strategy Consultants, London, UK

PHOTOGRAPHER: Jon O'Brien

DATE OF COMPLETION: July 1990

TARGET MARKET: Music and video customers, 25–40 years

PLACE OF SALE: Virgin Megastores

CLIENT'S BRIEF: To make the Megastore the pre-eminent music outlet and to create a shopping environment that would be as exciting and adrenalin-pumping as the music itself. To expose customers to the full range of products available in the Megastore and to exploit these to maximum effect.

DESIGN RATIONALE: Prior to the development of the 'Listening Stand' customers could only listen to one record store-wide: that chosen by the store's DJ over the PA system. 20/20 developed the means by which customers could listen to and then buy some of the 60,000 music titles available in the Megastores. Having listened, the customer can pick up the product from the adjacent display and head for the cash till. The 'look' of the 'Listening Stand' was designed so as to blend with the rest of the 'Megastore' scheme.

Reebok
BLACKTOP
TM

Training Shoes

CLIENT: Footlocker/Reebok, Houghton, MA, USA

DESCRIPTION OF PRODUCT: Display stand

DESIGNER: Medallion Associates, New York, USA

PLACE OF SALE: Footlocker (Athletic Shoe Retailer), USA

CLIENT'S BRIEF: The 'Blacktop' display was designed specifically for basketball shoes and had to reflect the fact that the shoes are worn primarily on outdoor courts.

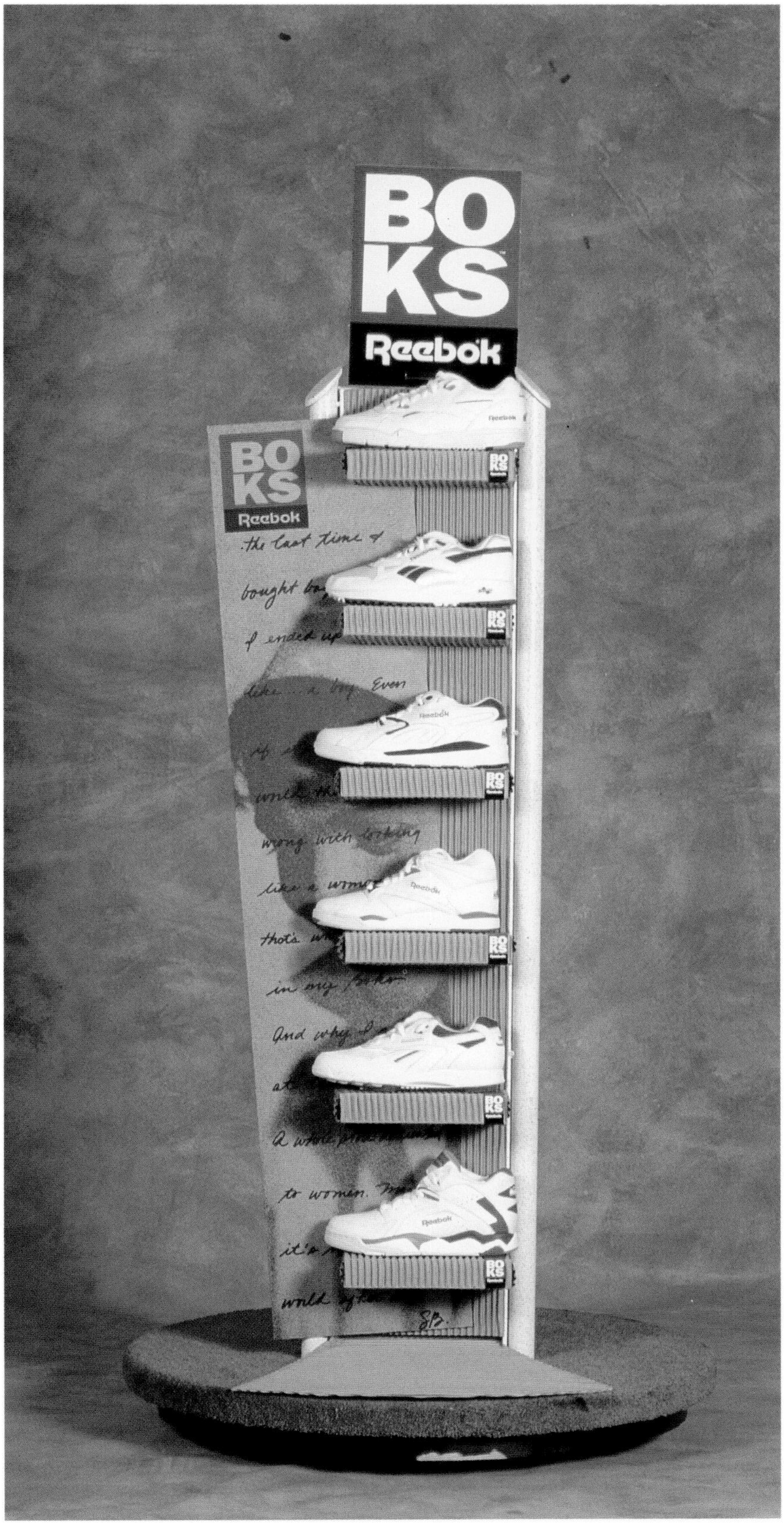

Counter-top promotions Anyone who has ever walked into the perfume department of a large department store will, once they have run the gauntlet of the sweet-talking demonstrators relentlessly spraying wrists with the latest scent, be aware of hundreds of immaculate little structures that cover every inch of the counter-top.

Having once worked on such structures, I am aware of the amount of time and care that is spent by the designers in trying to cram as creatively as possible the required number of lipsticks, blushers or eye-shadows into the smallest space, and at the same time present them in a new way that follows the advertising theme and includes the corporate logo and the fashion photography.

The examples I have chosen in this chapter seem to achieve these aims in effortless and inventive variety, and they also integrate the product in a considered and relevant way. But also included is a variety of other counter-top product categories from sunglasses and watches to trainers and jeans.

TRACTION PRODUCTIONS
DUCTIONS
TRACTION PRODUCTIONS

dual action
conditioning
shampoo
shampooing
conditionneur
double action
R E A C T

React

CLIENT: Marks & Spencer PLC, London, UK

DESIGNER: Michael Sheridan & Co Ltd, Leicester, UK

DATE OF COMPLETION: 1989

TARGET MARKET: Men, middle/upper market, 16–45 years

PLACE OF SALE: Marks & Spencer retail outlets

CLIENT'S BRIEF: To provide a testing facility to support the launch of a new range of male toiletries to be sold within M&S outlets in UK, Europe and export markets. The design of the tester bar had to reflect the designer image of the pack design.

DESIGN RATIONALE: The size constraints were important to ensure siting on M&S shelves. Design, materials and finishes selected and specified had to appeal to the design-aware target market. Interchangeable product location had to be designed to accommodate future range additions or changes.

Golden Beauty

CLIENT: Helena Rubenstein, Boulogne, France

DESCRIPTION OF PRODUCT: Display for Golden Beauty suncare products

DESIGNER: Raison Pure, Paris, France

DATE OF COMPLETION: March 1992

TARGET MARKET: Selective

PLACE OF SALE: Department stores and perfumeries

CLIENT'S BRIEF: To make a display for the launch of the Golden Beauty suncare line with a Tuscan, elegant, refined and luxurious backdrop.

DESIGN RATIONALE: To create a background for the product which conveys the image and the particular line in an imaginative way.

Rouge Forever Lipstick

CLIENT: Helena Rubinstein, Boulogne, France

DESCRIPTION OF PRODUCT: Large stone wall with small niches for product

DESIGNER: Raison Pure, Paris, France

DATE OF COMPLETION: January 1992

PLACE OF SALE: Department stores and perfumeries

CLIENT'S BRIEF: To provide a window display for the Rouge Forever lipstick.

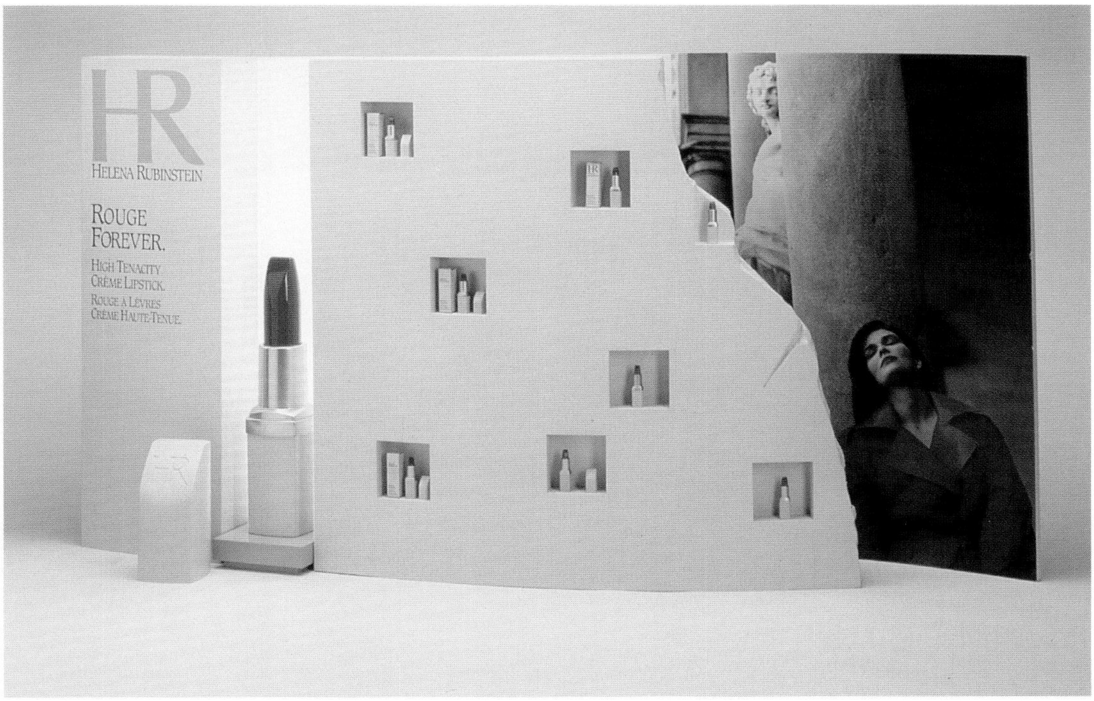

Rapport

CLIENT: Shulton (GB) Ltd – (Debbie Rayner), Wokingham, Berkshire, UK

DESCRIPTION OF PRODUCT: Rapport merchandizer (counter-top pack-display stand)

DESIGNER: Kate Merrifield; Art Director: Julian Money, Pethick & Money, London, UK

DATE OF COMPLETION: September 1990

TARGET MARKET: 18–25 male

PLACE OF SALE: Chemists' shops

CLIENT'S BRIEF: To produce a merchandizer that can accommodate different types and combinations of product and sales promotion material.

DESIGN RATIONALE: To emulate the design of the bottle in the design of the merchandizer, through the use of subtle curvature and a matt black finish.

No 7 Make-up Range

CLIENT: The Boots Company Ltd, Nottingham, UK
DESCRIPTION OF PRODUCT: Display stand
DESIGNER: KMD Marketing, Leicester, UK
DATE OF COMPLETION: 1992
TARGET MARKET: Female: mid-20s plus
PLACE OF SALE: Boots retail outlets
CLIENT'S BRIEF: To create a monthly promotion to introduce a new colour scheme for beauty products.

Rose Cardin

CLIENT: Cardin, Paris, France

DESCRIPTION OF PRODUCT: Metal, plastic and textiles display stand

DESIGNER: Pat PLV, Puteaux, France

DATE OF COMPLETION: October 1990

PLACE OF SALE: Perfumeries

PARFUMS
Rose Cardin
Rose Cardin

Shiseido Make-up Range

CLIENT: Shiseido, Paris, France

DESCRIPTION OF PRODUCT: Display units

DESIGNER: International Operations Division, Shiseido, Tokyo, Japan

TARGET MARKET: Women 25+

PLACE OF SALE: Department stores and pharmacies

SHISEIDO
Eye Shadow
Compact Foundation
Stick Foundation

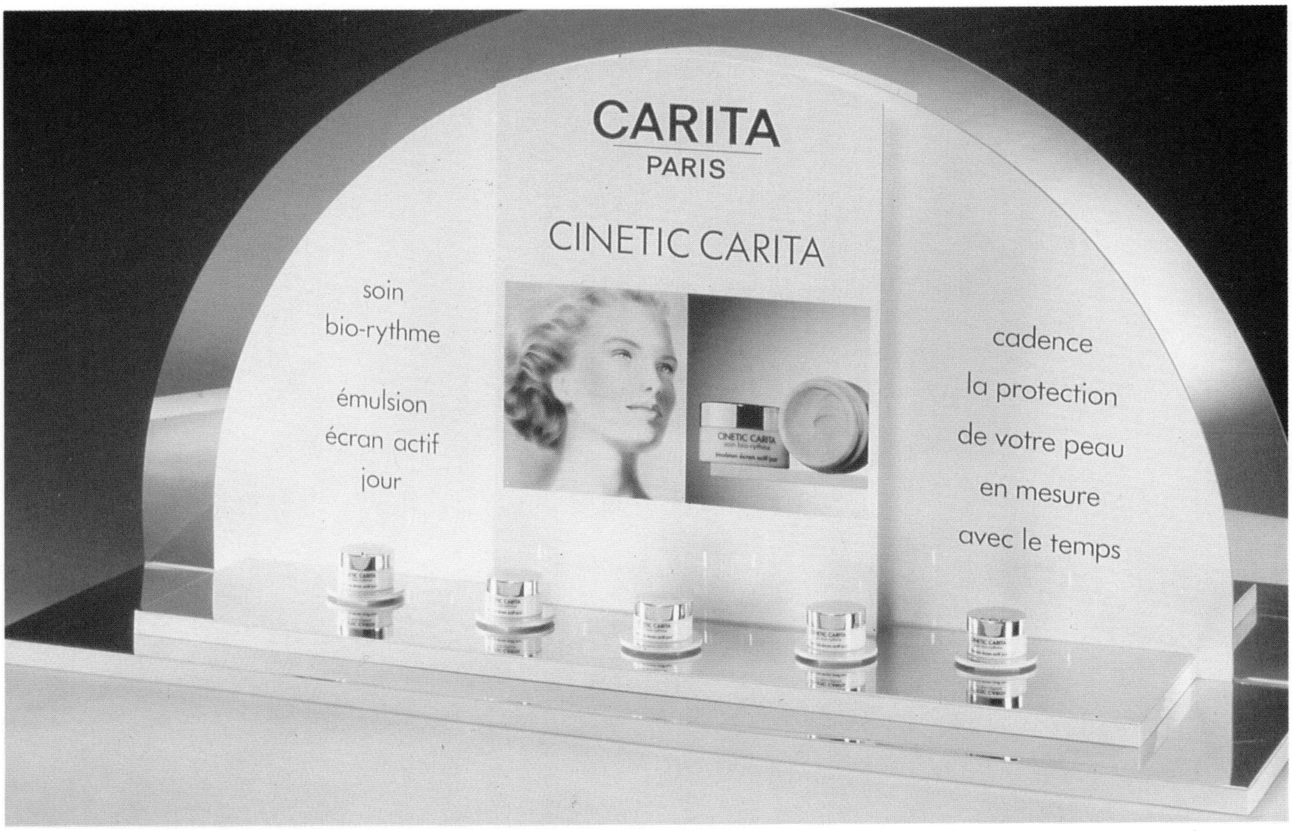

Carita

CLIENT: Carita, Paris, France

DESIGNER: PLV Services – MICAP, Noisy le Grand, France

DATE OF COMPLETION: 1992

TARGET MARKET: Women 25+

PLACE OF SALE: Perfumeries and department stores

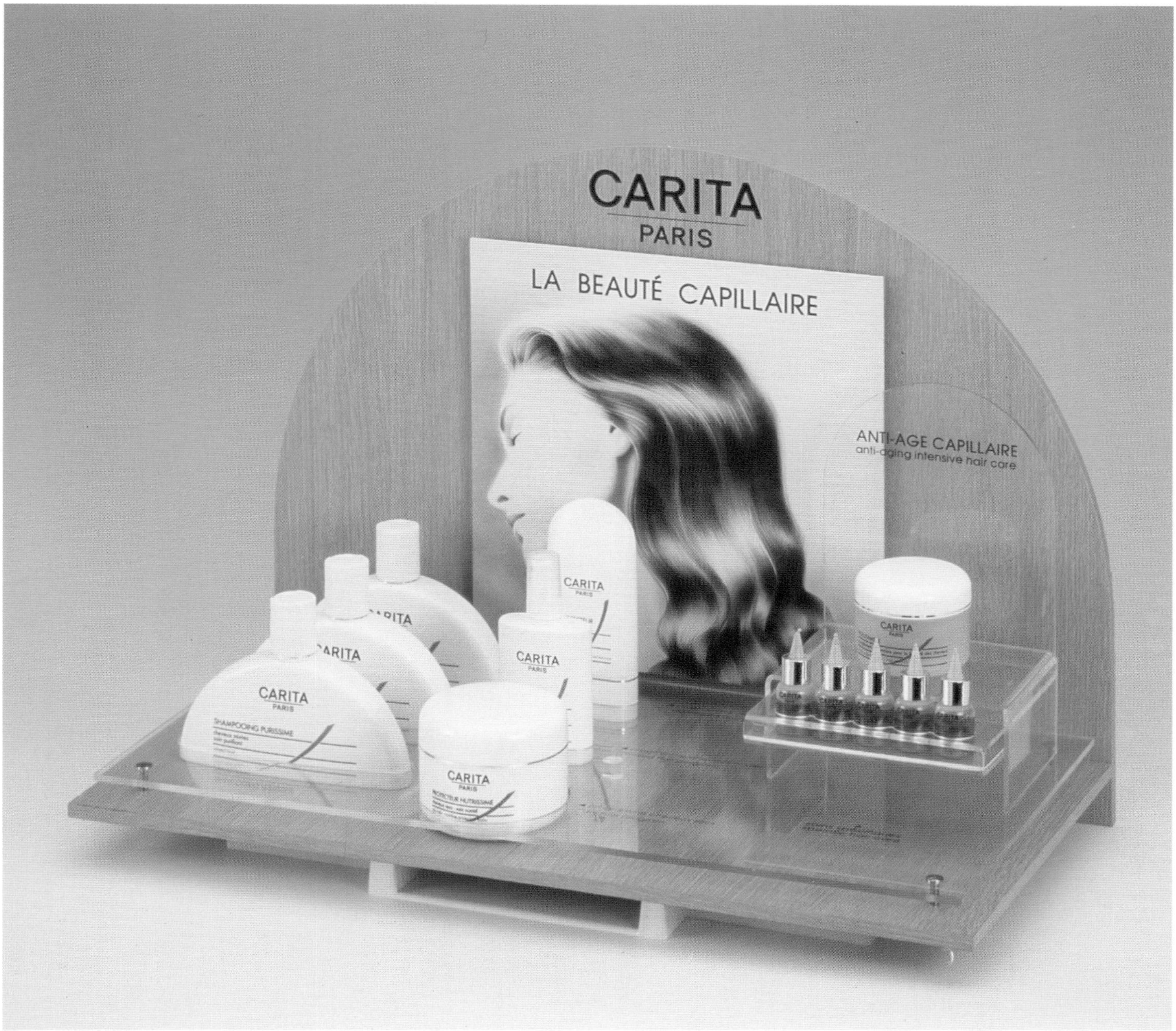
CARITA
PARIS
LA BEAUTÉ CAPILLAIRE
ANTI-AGE CAPILLAIRE
anti-aging intensive hair care
CARITA
PARIS
SHAMPOOING PURISSIME
CARITA
PARIS
PROTECTEUR NUTRISSIME

Shiseido

CLIENT: Shiseido, Paris, France

DESIGNER: PLV Services – MICAP, Noisy le Grand, France

DATE OF COMPLETION: 1992

TARGET MARKET: Women 25+

PLACE OF SALE: Perfumeries and department stores

SHISEIDO
SHISEIDO

ténéré
paco rabanne

Teneré; Calandre

CLIENT: Paco Rabanne, Paris, France

DESIGNER: PLV Services MICAP, Noisy le Grand, France

DATE OF COMPLETION: 1992

TARGET MARKET: Ténéré: men 25+;

Calandre: women 25+

PLACE OF SALE: Perfumeries and department stores

Obsession Tester Counter Units

CLIENT: Calvin Klein Cosmetics, New York, USA

DESCRIPTION OF PRODUCT: Injection-moulded in polycarbonate, UV silkscreen for fragrance resistance; fabricated acrylic templates.

DESIGNER: Consumer Promotions, Inc, New York, USA

DATE OF COMPLETION: July 1990

TARGET MARKET: Female and male

PLACE OF SALE: Retail department stores

CLIENT'S BRIEF: The objective of this display programme was to develop a series of displays to present Obsession Men's and Obsession Women's testers, on counter. Four displays were required: Men's Deluxe, Men's Single Tester, Women's Deluxe, and Women's Single Tester. The design had to follow the lines of the product packaging, conveying a soft, sophisticated feeling. The materials used to manufacture these displays had to look first class, and the displays had to be of the highest quality.

DESIGN RATIONALE: The design of these displays reflects the styling of the primary packages, yielding soft and curved shapes. All units feature injection-moulded base and header, to provide a constant high-quality finish. Material compatability, often a problem with fragrances, was solved using a special polycarbonate resin, which is highly resistant to attack by fragrances while also providing a deep lustre and rich colour.

OBSESSION
Calvin Klein
OBSESSION
FOR MEN
AFTER SHAVE BALM
Calvin Klein
OBSESSION
Calvin Klein
OBSESSION
Calvin Klein

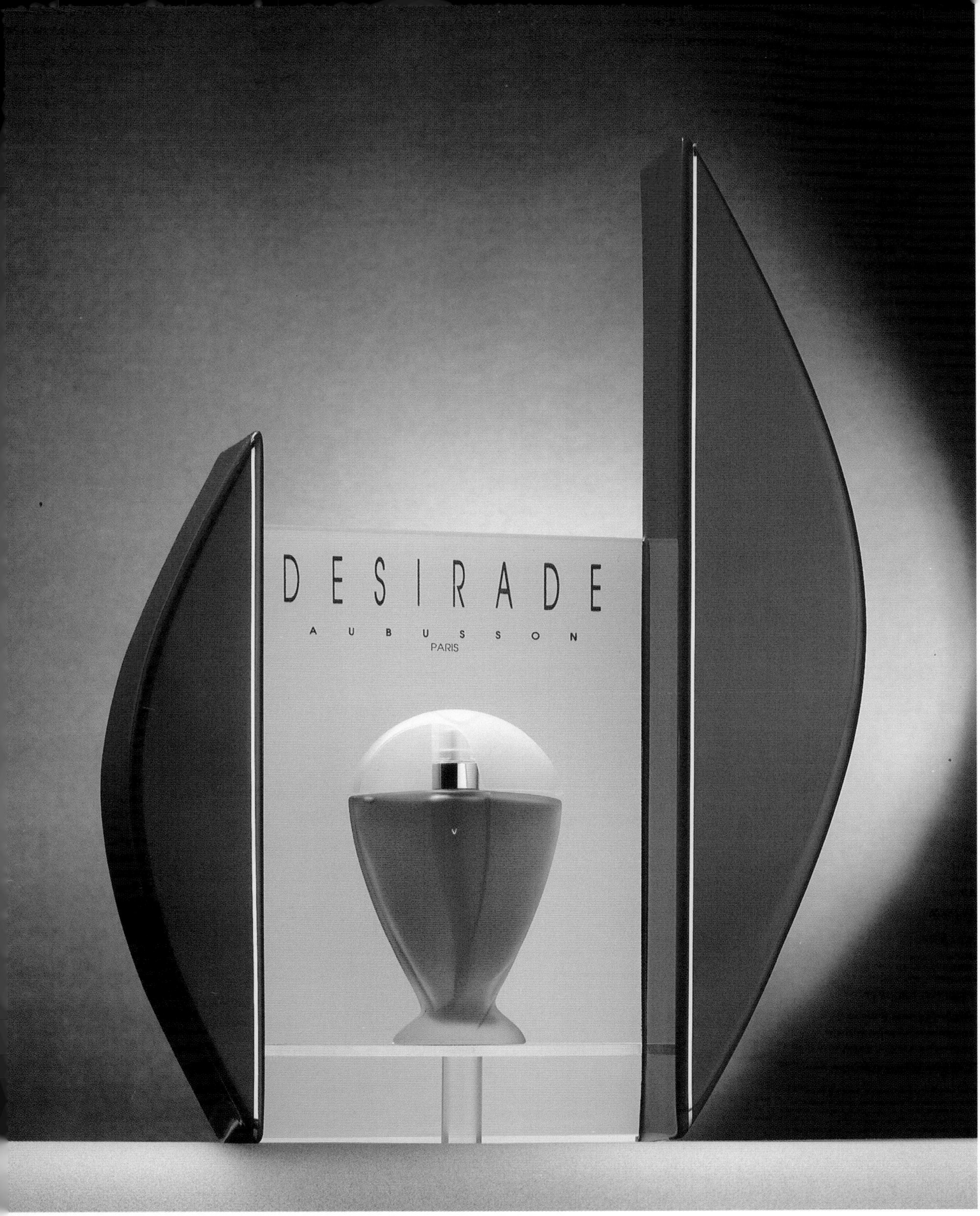

Désirade

CLIENT: Parfums Aubusson, St Germain-en-Laye, France

DESCRIPTION OF PRODUCT: Plastic display stand

DESIGNER: Pat PLV, Puteaux, France

DATE OF COMPLETION: Beginning of 1991

PLACE OF SALE: Perfumeries

Ombre Subtile Eyeshadow

CLIENT: Lancôme, Paris, France

DESCRIPTION OF PRODUCT: Display and tester unit, principally manufactured from injection-moulded polystyrene. Size: 43cm × 42cm × 26cm

DESIGNER: Studio DM Design, Paris and Creative Unit of Lancôme International Merchandizing

DATE OF COMPLETION: Spring 1992

TARGET MARKET: Female – sophisticated users of colour cosmetics

PLACE OF SALE: Department stores and perfumeries

CLIENT'S BRIEF: To create a display and tester unit for two new ranges of eyeshadows. They had to reflect the refinement of the product; feature the advertising visual for the product; show the new compact and test both ranges of product; the product testers had to be easily renewable.

DESIGN RATIONALE: To feature the existing Lancôme make-up corporate shades and colour for merchandizing.

Display Stands for Lancôme

CLIENT: Lancôme, Paris, France

DESCRIPTION OF PRODUCT: Display stands and tester units for range of Lancôme products

DESIGNER: Studio DM Design, Paris and Creative Unit of Lancôme International Marketing

DATE OF COMPLETION: 1992

TARGET MARKET: Sophisticated panels

PLACE OF SALE: Department stores and perfumeries

LANCÔME
L'ART DU TEINT
PARFAIT
Effet Mat
Effet Mat
RÉSULTAT
NATUREL COUVRANT

Trésor
LANCÔME
PARIS

S
NAIL
GLASS

Trucco Cosmetics

CLIENT: Sebastian, Woodland Hills, California, USA

DESCRIPTION OF PRODUCT: Trucco Cosmetic, point-of-sale display is constructed from fabricated acrylic and a vacuum-formed tray/insert. Size: 16in × 14in × 2in.

DESIGNER: Stuart Karten Design, Marina del Rey, California, USA

ILLUSTRATOR OR PHOTOGRAPHER: Henry Blackham

DATE OF COMPLETION: 1988

TARGET MARKET: Females aged 19 to 65

PLACE OF SALE: Professional hair salons

CLIENT'S BRIEF: The client needed a counter-top point-of-sale that could easily be changed every four months. It needed to draw attention to the product line and to excite the customer.

DESIGN RATIONALE: A simple black acrylic display was created that accepts a black vacuum-formed insert. The insert changed every four months as new colours and products were highlighted. It needed to be easy to replace. The insert design and form had to change with each new introduction. The forms would be representational of the concept for that season (in other words natural colors would be represented with natural forms, water, stone etc.).

Ingrid Millet Shop Window Display

CLIENT: Ingrid Millet/Groupe Revillon, Paris, France

DESCRIPTION OF PRODUCT: Display, 1 × 2m

DESIGNER: Jean-Pierre Toth, Méthacryl, Paris, France

DATE OF COMPLETION: 1989

PLACE OF SALE: Ingrid Millet authorized shops

CLIENT'S BRIEF: To promote solar products of the Perle de Caviar range, and to evoke the sea, sun and water.

DESIGN RATIONALE: Atmosphere of the sea and sun represented by the sails of the stylized deckchair with white and yellow as predominant colours.

Ingrid Millet Product Support

CLIENT: Ingrid Millet/Groupe Revillon, Paris, France

DESIGNER: Jean-Pierre Toth, Méthacryl, Suresnes, France

DATE OF COMPLETION: 1990

PLACE OF SALE: Ingrid Millet shops

CLIENT'S BRIEF: To promote a range of products – Nature Active luxury beauty products – to recreate the atmosphere of a beauty institute: clean and sober.

DESIGN RATIONALE: To recreate the atmosphere of a beauty institute in-store and a situation for a luxury product

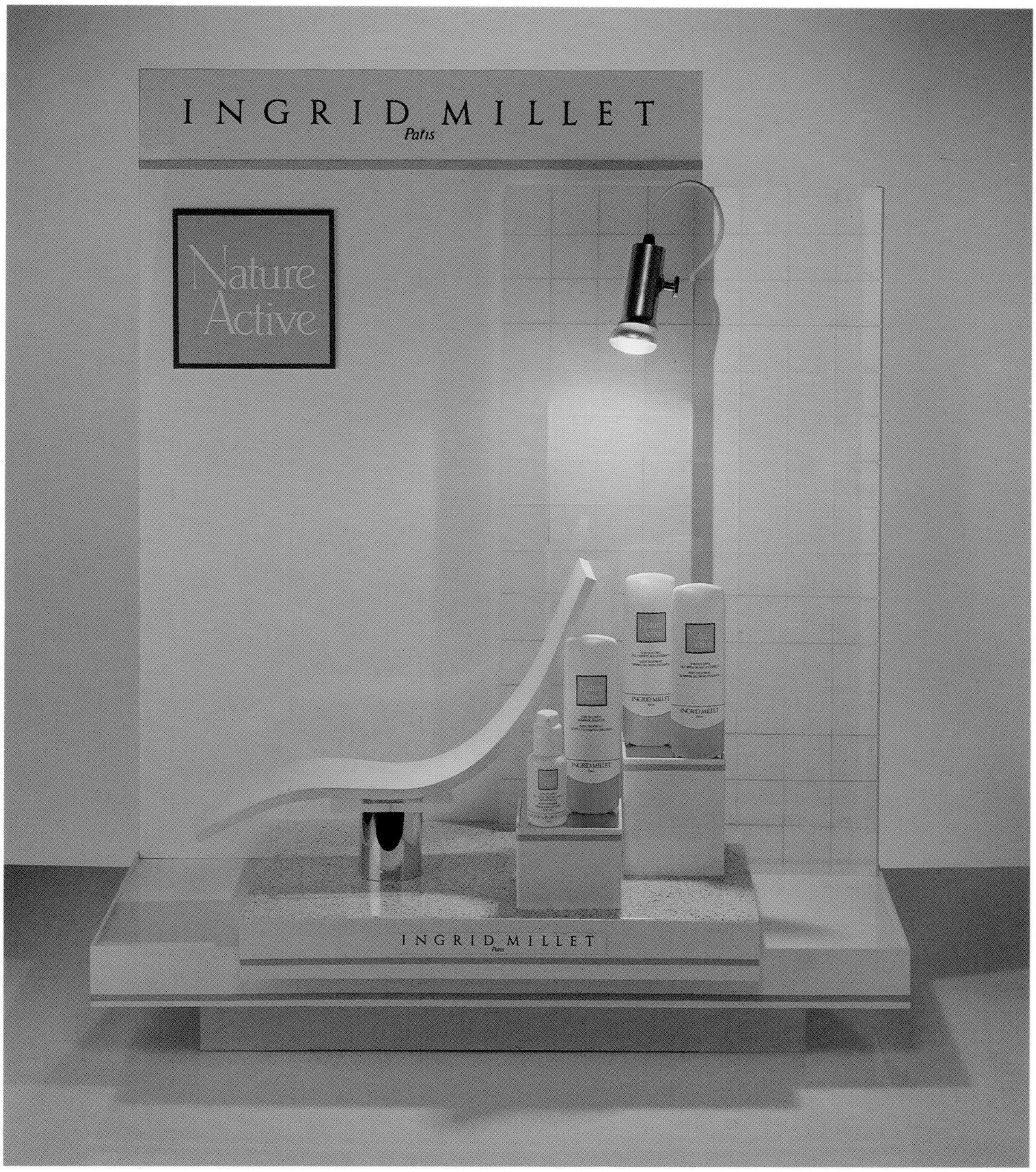

Window Visual Support

CLIENT: Caron/Groupe Revillon, Paris, France

DESIGNER: Jean-Pierre Toth, Méthacryl, Paris, France

DATE OF COMPLETION: 1990

PLACE OF SALE: Caron retail shops

CLIENT'S BRIEF: To evoke travel, adventure, discovery – reflect the product and press release (poster)

Shiseido Window Display

CLIENT: Shiseido, Paris, France

DESCRIPTION OF PRODUCT: Shiseido make-up range

DESIGNER: Jean-Pierre Toth, Méthacryl, Suresnes, France

SHISEIDO
LE MAQUILLAGE
SHISEIDO
SHISEIDO
IMMUABLE PAR SERGE LUTENS
SHISEIDO

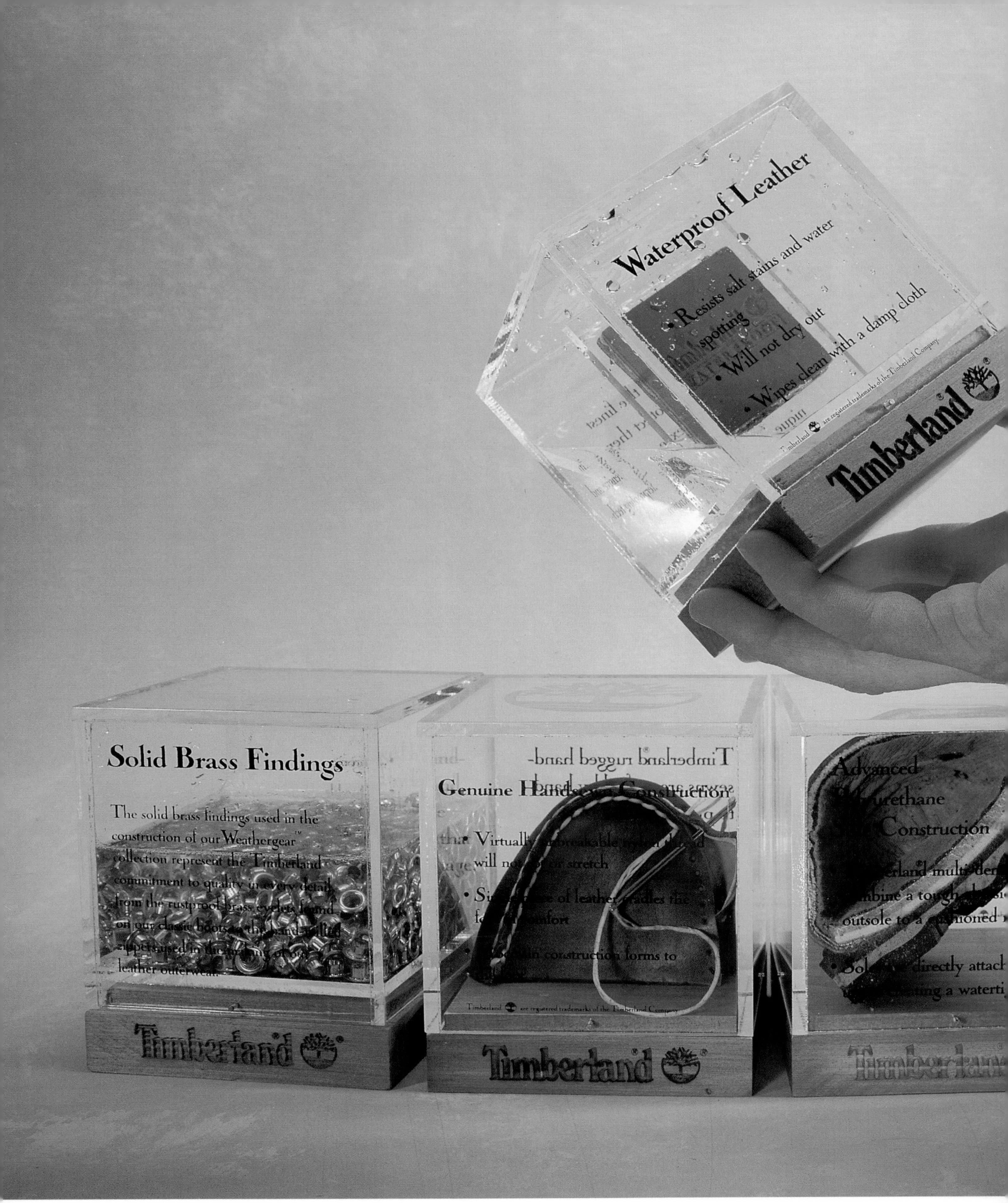
Waterproof Leather
• Resists salt stains and water spotting
• Will not dry out
• Wipes clean with a damp cloth
Timberland
Solid Brass Findings
The solid brass findings used in the
construction of our Weathergear™
Timberland
Timberland
Timberland

Timberland Interactive Cubes

CLIENT: The Timberland Company, Hampton, NH, USA

DESCRIPTION OF PRODUCT: Timberland footwear display showing five component parts of footwear construction

DESIGNERS: Ron Tise, Vice President – Retail
Kevin McCarthy, Director of Store Design and Presentation, Jarvis Brecker, Project Manager, The Timberland Company

DATE OF COMPLETION: January 1992

TARGET MARKET: For discerning people who value the outdoors and their time in it.

PLACE OF SALE: Timberland Specialty Stores, independent footwear and clothing stores, department stores.

CLIENT'S BRIEF: To demonstrate, in an interactive way, the core equities of all Timberland products at the point of sale.

DESIGN RATIONALE: Timberland's most important achievement has been to design and develop quality footwear, clothing and accessories that last. Many of these products are developed using specific technologies that Timberland has helped pioneer over the last 35 years. These technologies, called Core Equities, are incorporated in most Timberland footwear, clothing and accessories. They consist of waterproof leather, waterproof breathable fabrics and linings, handmade quality workmanship, durable corrosion-proof hardware and comfortable, 100% waterproof direct-attach footwear soles.

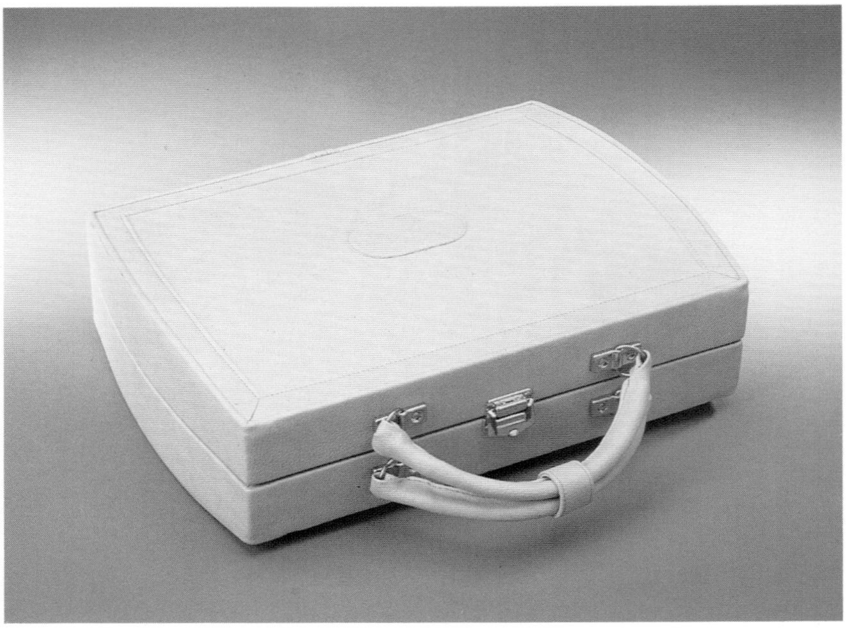

Sample Suitcase for Golden Beauty Range

CLIENT: Helena Rubinstein, Boulogne, France

DESCRIPTION OF PRODUCT: Portable showcase for Golden Beauty range

DESIGNER: Raison Pure, Paris, France

DATE OF COMPLETION: March 1992

TARGET MARKET: Selective

PLACE OF SALE: Department stores and perfumeries

CLIENT'S BRIEF: To create a sample case for the sales people which was both elegant and practical, and conveyed the image of the product.

DESIGN RATIONALE: A suitcase in which the warm colours of the product were represented in the rich and elegant material of the case itself.

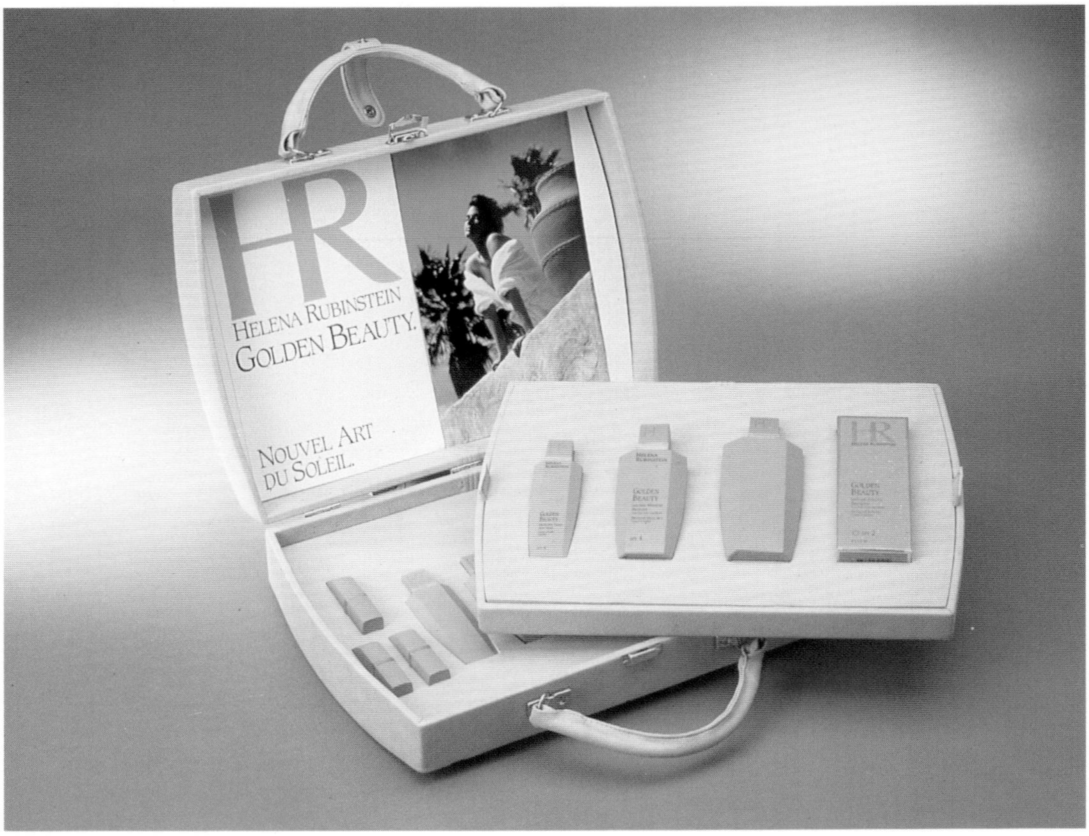

Lauren Product Glorifier

CLIENT: Cosmair, Inc/Ralph Lauren, New York, USA

DESCRIPTION OF PRODUCT: Bird's-eye maple, genuine hand-sewn leather, 22K gold plate valve and catch pan, custom-manufactured strap stays, engraved mirror, articulated drawer action.

DESIGNER: Consumer Promotion, Inc, New York, USA

DATE OF COMPLETION: March 1988

TARGET MARKET: Female

PLACE OF SALE: Retail department stores

CLIENT'S BRIEF: A campaign was established to enhance the richness of the Ralph Lauren 'Lauren' look. The image of country style and elegance was expressed through the use of wood and leather, giving the entire line a specific feeling and tone. These displays heightened customer awareness of a new look that translates into the natural beauty of the outdoors. It conveys the feelings of down-to-earth, fresh air and country life associated with the Lauren woman.

DESIGN RATIONALE: Consumer Promotions produced these displays to accomplish a unique and fine piece of well-crafted wood cabinet and mirror box reminiscent of days gone by when quality pieces were built to last – a key factor in the parameters of the well-established ethics of the Ralph Lauren look. This look readily identifies these displays as a Ralph Lauren design statement.

Sunglasses Display

CLIENT: IDC, Marseille, France

DESCRIPTION OF PRODUCT: The base and central part of this display are made of enamelled wood. The background is of aluminium, the central decoration is made out of polystyrene mirror. The holders of the sunglasses are of rubber foam with metallic pins in the inside and tips of enamelled wood. Dimensions are: 70 × 40 × 20cm.

DESIGNER: RS Creation, Montreuil, France

DATE OF COMPLETION: 1989

TARGET MARKET: Purchasers of sunglasses

PLACE OF SALE: Opticians and gift shops

CLIENT'S BRIEF: To create a counter and window display, permitting the display of 12 pairs of glasses. The style of IDC is voluntarily very fashionable, but in a high price zone: the display was supposed to strengthen this image.

DESIGN RATIONALE: This brief was translated into a 'look' that is both actual and 'retro'. The use of materials that are at the same time traditional, luxurious and high-tech reinforces this element.

Essilor Glasses

CLIENT: Essilor, Joinville-le-Pont, France

DESCRIPTION OF PRODUCT: A display composed of a base of polyurethane foam representing the graphics of a Zen Japanese garden on which were fixed three vertical moulded and tinted wooden elements. These elements are perforated in order to receive small plexiglas tubes which support the glasses. Dimensions are: 50 × 40 × 35cm.

DESIGNER: RS Creation, Montreuil, France

DATE OF COMPLETION: April 1990

TARGET MARKET: Opticians

PLACE OF SALE: Specialized retailers

CLIENT'S BRIEF: To create a display for a new style of Essilor glasses, dedicated to city customers. The display was supposed to carry the more or less high-tech image of these targeted consumers.

DESIGN RATIONALE: As a symbol of the urban universe, three buildings were chosen for the design, which has a plain and restrained style, but is also tough and sophisticated (hence the use of the tinted and varnished wood).

Killer Loop Sunglass Display

CLIENT: Bausch & Lomb, Rochester, NY, USA

DESCRIPTION OF PRODUCT: The 'Killer loop' rope cable and sheet steel product holding display

DESIGNER: Arnell-Bickford Associates, New York, USA

MAKER: Thomson-Leeds Co. Inc., New York, USA

DATE OF COMPLETION: Summer 1990

TARGET MARKET: United States

PLACE OF SALE: Exclusive sporting goods, optical, speciality and department stores

CLIENT'S BRIEF: 'Killer loop', the term surfers use to describe a perfect physical performance on a cresting ocean wave, also captures the spirit of a display programme, for Bausch & Lomb's new high-tech, high-performance 'killer loop' line of sunglasses.

DESIGN RATIONALE: The 'killer loop' concept, using rope cable and sheet steel, transmits a sense of kinetic energy and provides a practical, product holding display.

Traction Production Glasses

CLIENT: Victor Gros, Traction Production, Clairvaux les Lacs, France

DESCRIPTION OF PRODUCT: Metal display stand

DESIGNER: Pat PLV, Puteaux, France

DATE OF COMPLETION: End of 1990

PLACE OF SALE: Opticians

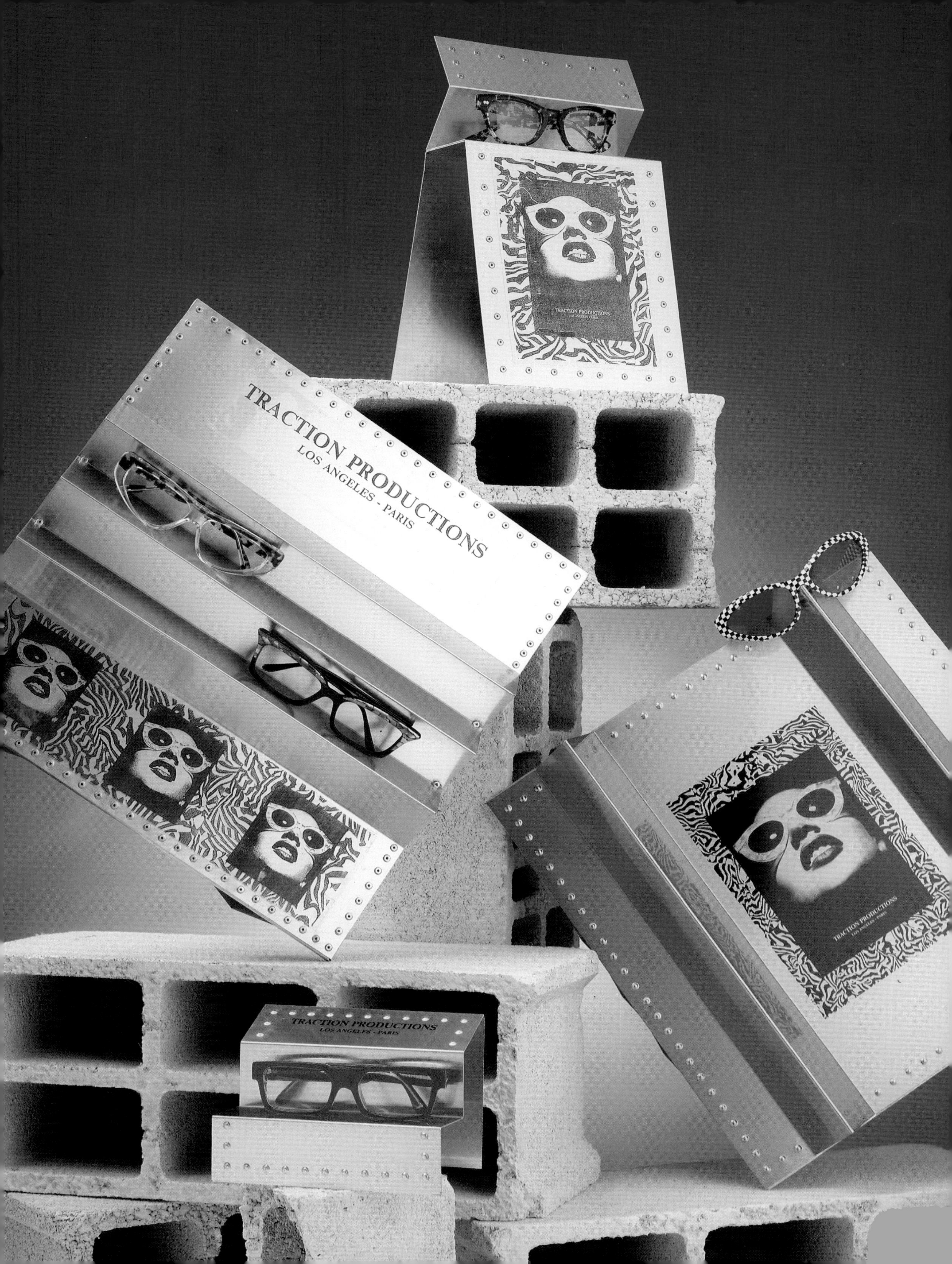
TRACTION PRODUCTIONS
LOS ANGELES - PARIS
TRACTION PRODUCTIONS
LOS ANGELES - PARIS

Polaroid Sunglasses

CLIENT: Polaroid Sunglasses, Polaroid Corporation, London, UK

DESCRIPTION OF PRODUCT: "Image" Sunglasses packaging and point-of-sale material

DESIGNER: John Rushworth, Theirry Goignat, John Powner, Pentagram Design Ltd, London, UK

DATE OF COMPLETION: 1987

CLIENT'S BRIEF: The packaging and point-of-sale material for this exclusive range of Polaroid "Image" sunglasses emphasized the superior quality of the product and highlighted the high specification design. The sunglasses themselves were designed by Pentragram partner Kenneth Grange.

Polaroid Promotion

CLIENT: Polaroid Corporation, London, UK

DESCRIPTION OF PRODUCT: Business and professional packaging, point-of-sale and promotional material

DESIGNER: John Rushworth, Bob Mytton, Pentagram Design Ltd, London, UK

DATE OF COMPLETION: 1989

CLIENT'S BRIEF: Speed, confidentiality and accuracy make Polaroid instant film valuable for business and professional use, and as an effective means of communication. New packaging, point-of-sale and promotional material was designed to promote this aspect of Polaroid.

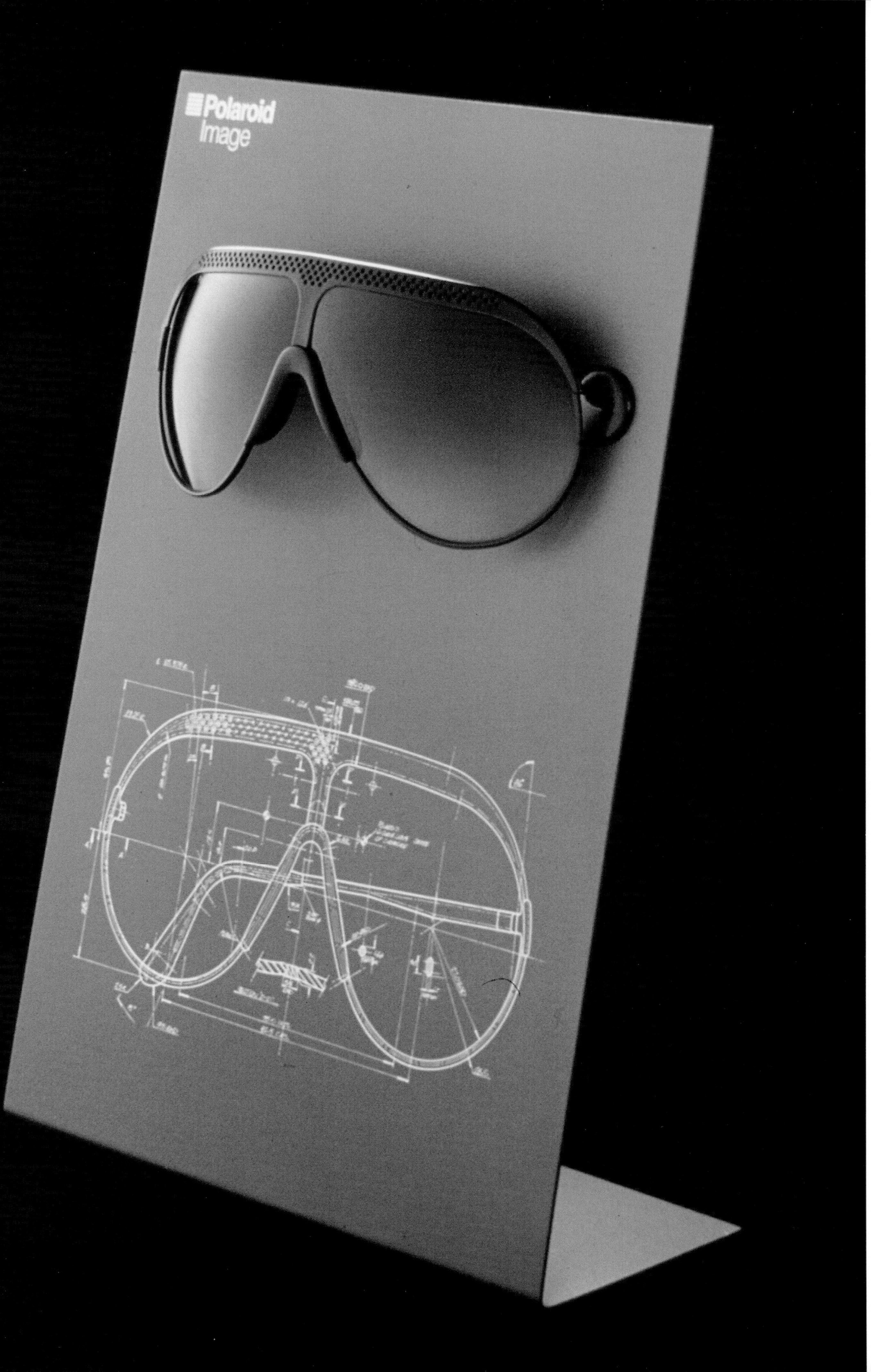
Polaroid
Image

Porto Quinta do Noval

CLIENT: Expression F C A, Bordeaux, France

DESCRIPTION OF PRODUCT: Lacquered wood, cardboard and vacuum-forming. Dimensions: height 800mm; width 600mm; depth 400mm.

DESIGNER: Prisme, Suresnes, France

DATE OF COMPLETION: June 1991

TARGET MARKET: Port drinkers of any age

PLACE OF SALE: Wine stores and high-quality food shops

CLIENT'S BRIEF: To create a display counter for 'Quinta do Noval' port that conveys the following messages to the public: Port wine is a product of Portugal; Quinta do Noval is an upper class port. The best way to taste and appreciate port wine is by using a decanter to aerate and let out the aroma.

DESIGN RATIONALE: The decanter (an indispensible item for appreciating a good port wine) was made the star of the display by enlarging it to one and a half times its usual size. Each main element is immediately identifiable with Portugal: 'the azulejos' and the richness of their decor and design are seen in a beautiful back drop representing a vineyard. Keeping guard in front of the vines are two bottles of port. One of these is deliberately higher than the other to make it understood that not all 'Quinta do Noval' port wines are the same.

Class Affair

CLIENT: O.D.L.M. Façonnable, Champagne au Mont d'Or, France

DESCRIPTION OF PRODUCT: Exotic woods; acrylic mirror; injected-moulded plastic sheet; size: height 430mm; width 590mm; depth 300mm

DESIGNER: Prisme, Suresnes, France

DATE OF COMPLETION: September 1991

TARGET MARKET: Top-end of the range customers, male and female

PLACE OF SALE: Opticians

CLIENT'S BRIEF: To create a high-quality display for the launch of a new line of tortoiseshell-rimmed regular glasses 'Class Affair'.

DESIGN RATIONALE: In Europe the use of wood and Art Deco style are two important trends in interior architecture and decoration, so it was decided to create this environment on a small scale in order to reach the potential consumer. The feeling of fine furniture spotlights the star product in the line. The structure incorporating exotic woods of both light and dark tones underlines the concept of quality. The back mirror gives a feeling of spaciousness.

Rucanor Shoe Display

CLIENT: Rucanor BV, The Netherlands

DESCRIPTION OF PRODUCT: Acrylic, lisa, screenprint

DESIGNER: Alrec PoS Design, The Netherlands

DATE OF COMPLETION: 1991

TARGET MARKET: Sports shoe wearers

PLACE OF SALE: Sports shoe shops

CLIENT'S BRIEF: To design an exclusive shoe display for the introduction of new Rucanor sport shoes.

Sony Headphones

CLIENT: Sony UK Ltd, London, UK

DESIGNER: Alrec POS Design, Hillegorn, The Netherlands

SECRET
Sport is an Art
Rucanor

Best Direction

CLIENT: Best Direction Ltd., Greenford, Middlesex, UK

DESCRIPTION OF PRODUCT: Free-standing board with slot to hang one pair of jeans

DESIGNER: Big Active Ltd, London, UK

DATE OF COMPLETION: 1990

TARGET MARKET: Male, aged 20–40

PLACE OF SALE: High street fashion retail stores

CLIENT'S BRIEF: To design an item of point-of-sale which would display a pair of Best Direction jeans, with a simple construction that was also easy to use.

DESIGN RATIONALE: The point-of-sale item was developed on a theme for Best Direction entitled 'The Greatest Story Ever Told'. The old book design evoked a mood of classic nostalgia. The simple construction enabled the product to be very visible.

Puiforcat 'Normandy'

CLIENT: Puiforcat, La Plaine Saint Denis, France

DESCRIPTION OF PRODUCT: Lacquered wood; acrylic sheet; polyurethane foam; size: width 370mm; height 400mm; depth 380mm

DESIGNER: Prisme, Suresnes, France

DATE OF COMPLETION: November 1990

TARGET MARKET: Upper end of the range customers

PLACE OF SALE: Department stores and European speciality shops

CLIENT'S BRIEF: This place setting was specially designed for the steamship 'Normandy' in 1934. In 1991 it has been re-created for general sales. Puiforcat wanted a small display to emphasize the history of the design and to present the line.

DESIGN RATIONALE: To symbolize the steamship 'Normandy' in the clearest fashion, to show the elements of the design. The deck of the ship had to give the perfect presentation for the place setting. It had to be reminiscent of the real ship; the name is spotlighted on the 'bow' of the display. The two acrylic plates symbolize sea foam and waves breaking over the ship and show off the well-known logo 'Puiforcat'.

Little Cobbler

CLIENT: Bally, Paris, France

DESCRIPTION OF PRODUCT: Miniature display of cobbler

DESIGNER: Bally, Paris, France

PLACE OF SALE: Bally retail outlets

Trifari Tune-In Interactive Marketing Programme

CLIENT: Trifari, Inc., New York, NY, USA

DESCRIPTION OF PRODUCT: Trifari Tune-In Interactive Marketing Programme

DESIGNER: Trans World Marketing, East Rutherford, NJ, USA

DATE OF COMPLETION: June 1990

TARGET MARKET: Females

PLACE OF SALE: Department stores

CLIENT'S BRIEF: To educate Trifari consumers on the fundamental basics of accessorizing. To offer the opportunity to generate in-store excitement and multiple purchase of Trifari jewelry through special event promotion.

DESIGN RATIONALE: To launch the programme, three jewelry programmes were created: Face Shape, Neckline and Wardrobe Building Analysis. A full-colour Tune-In reference manual visually reinforces the interactive programme, enhances media advertising efforts and assists consumers in selecting from Trifari's 3,000+ jewelry styles.

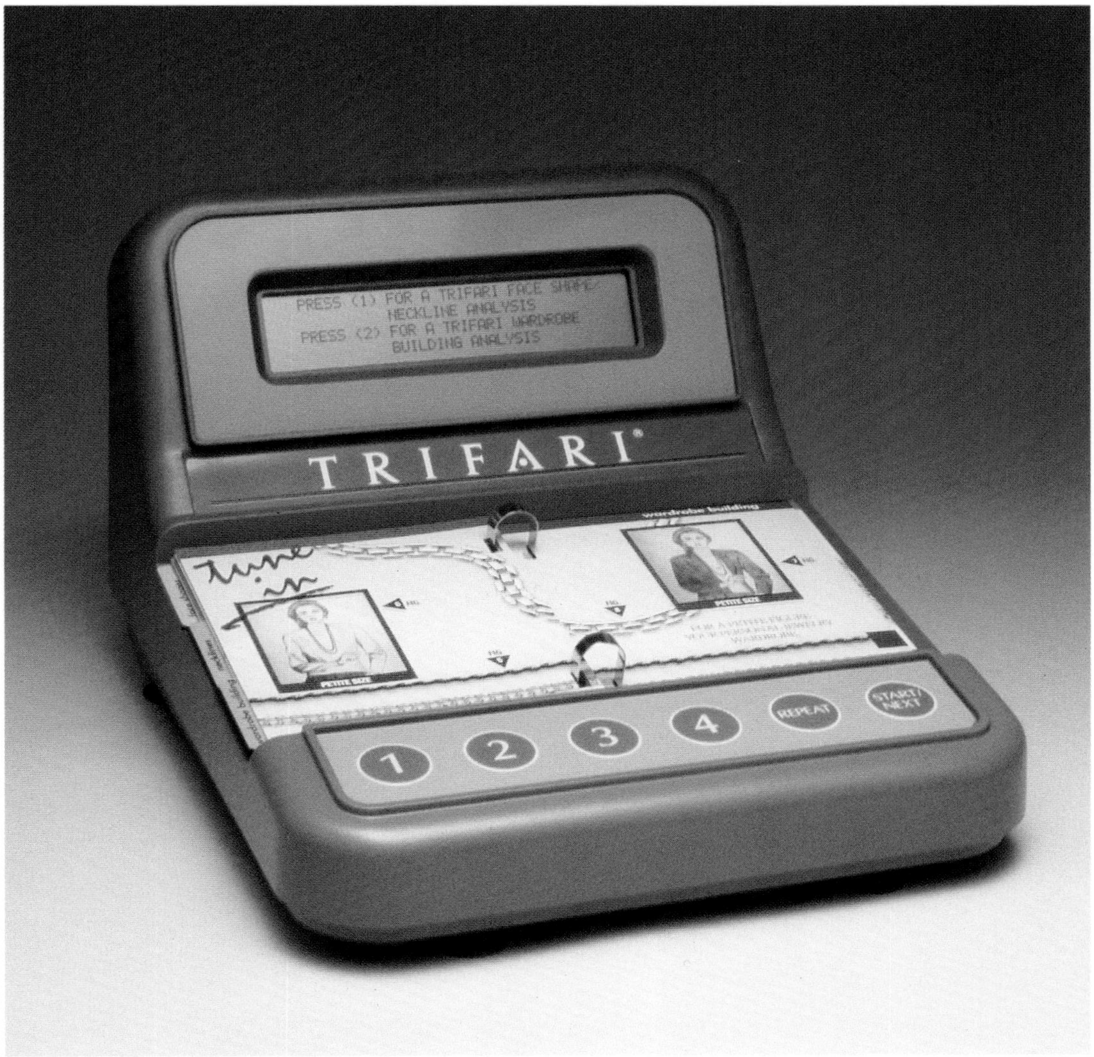

Boddington's Keg Bitter and Mild

CLIENT: Boddingtons Breweries Limited, Manchester, UK

DESCRIPTION OF PRODUCT: Countermounts in metal and bevelled glass

DESIGNER: Stephen Gibbons & Malcolm Swatridge, The Partners, London, UK

DATE OF COMPLETION: 1989

TARGET MARKET: Club and pub customers

PLACE OF SALE: Clubs, pubs, etc

CLIENT'S BRIEF: The countermounts had to be clearly seen both from the front and from an oblique view along the bar.

Beer Mats

CLIENT: Dryborough, Edinburgh, Scotland, UK

DESIGNERS: Stephen Gibbons, David Stuart, The Partners, London, UK

ILLUSTRATOR OR PHOTOGRAPHER: Mick Brownfield

DATE OF COMPLETION: 1987

TARGET MARKET: A broad cross-section of drinkers

PLACE OF SALE: Pubs

CLIENT'S BRIEF: To promote a new product at point-of-sale

DESIGN RATIONALE: The beer mats were designed to reflect a broad range of possible consumers, to create interest and to encourage their collection.

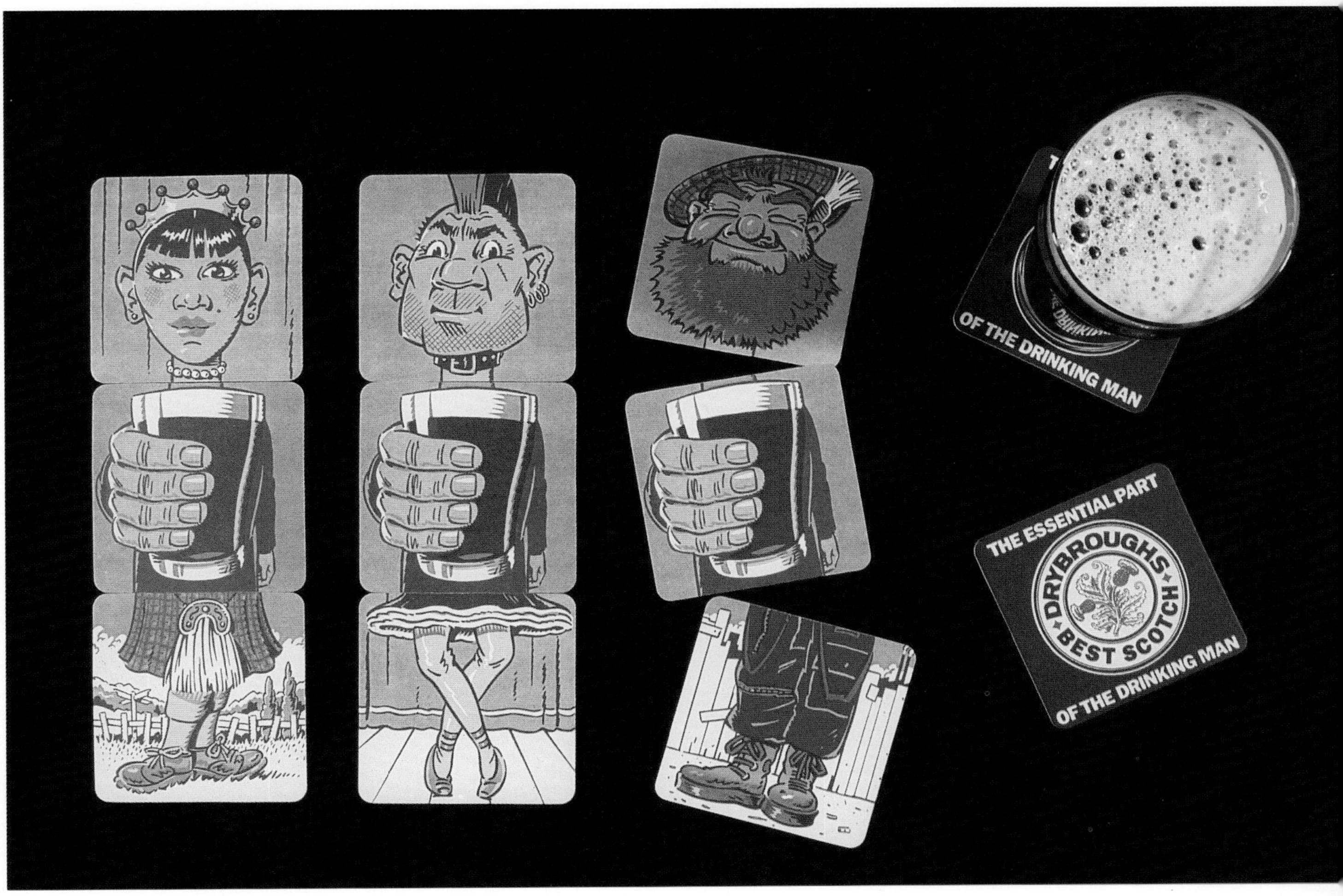

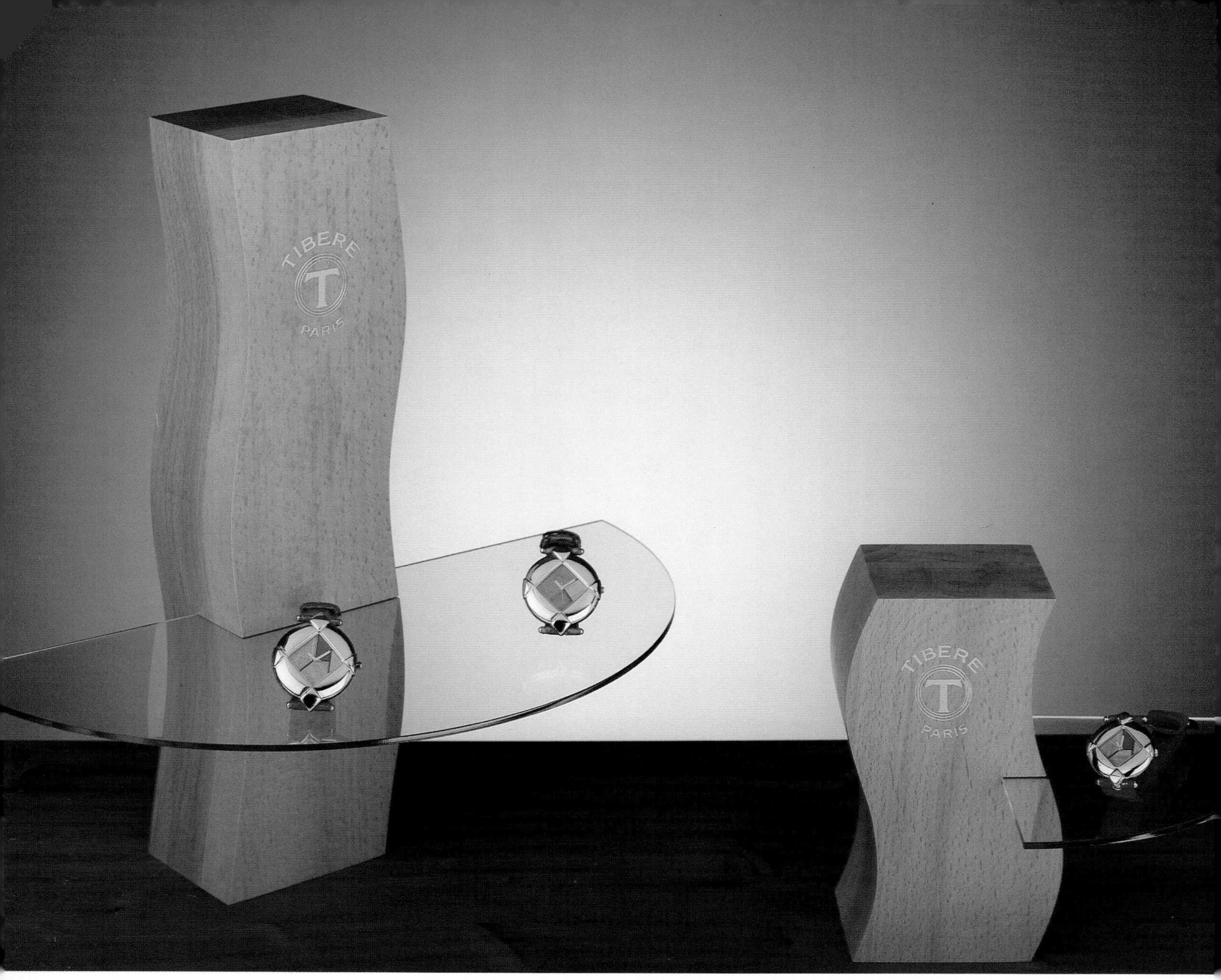

Tibere Watches

CLIENT: Tibere, Paris, France

DESCRIPTION OF PRODUCT: Wood and plastic display stand

DESIGNER: Pat PLV, Puteaux, France

DATE OF COMPLETION: End of 1991

PLACE OF SALE: Jeweller's shops

Sola Clip-ons

CLIENT: Sola Optical Pty Ltd, Adelaide, South Australia

DESCRIPTION OF PRODUCT: Structure for sunglasses

DESIGNER: John Nowland, Adelaide, South Australia

DATE OF COMPLETION: 1984

TARGET MARKET: Clients of optometrists and wearers of prescribed spectacles

PLACE OF SALE: Optometrists

CLIENT'S BRIEF: System to display maximum number of clip-on sunglasses, easily packed and assembled.

DESIGN RATIONALE: Simple, robust, visually interesting system to display clip-on sun lenses. To be located on sales counter in optometrists' offices.

Royal Blue Display

CLIENT: Royal Copenhagen, Copenhagen, Denmark

DESCRIPTION OF PRODUCT: Full-size three-winged display

DESIGNER: Royal Copenhagen, Denmark

DATE OF COMPLETION: Spring 1992

TARGET MARKET: Sweden, Italy, USA, UK, Japan and Germany

PLACE OF SALE: Porcelain retailers

CLIENT'S BRIEF: The three-winged display is part of a comprehensive range of point of sale material developed to support the international Royal Blue campaign from Royal Copenhagen Ltd in-store. The material is meant to supplement the unique beauty, craftsmanship and fine old traditions that lies behind the blue services from Royal Copenhagen.

DESIGN RATIONALE: The display enables the shop, with a relatively limited amount of space, to show the full context in which the products are best displayed. Combining the services with cutlery and glassware also produced by Royal Copenhagen in both a classical and a modern version for the younger generation stresses the versatile nature of the blue services.

ROYAL COPENHAGEN
ROYAL COPENHAGEN

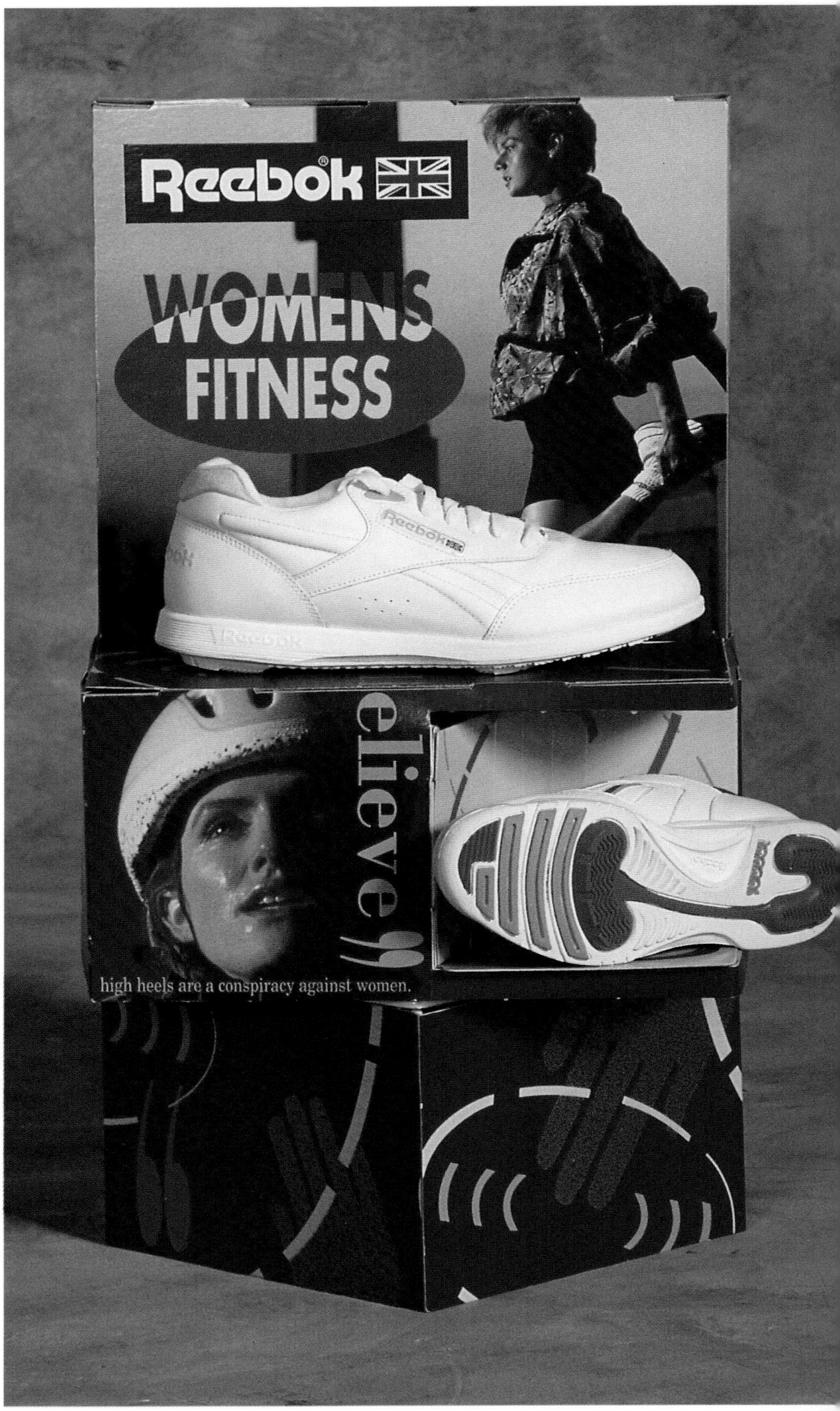

I Believe

CLIENT: Lady Footlocker, New York, USA, and Reebok, Stoughton, Massachusetts, USA

DESCRIPTION OF PRODUCT: 18pt board (approx 30 × 72cm)

DESIGNER: J P Terlizzi & Susan Bettancourt, Medallion Associates, New York, USA

DATE OF COMPLETION: April/May 1992

TARGET MARKET: Females aged 19–34

PLACE OF SALE: Lady Footlocker (athletic footwear and apparel retailer exclusively for women)

CLIENT'S BRIEF: To design a point-of-sale unit that would be utilized on an existing store fixture. The display had to tie into existing Reebok TV and print campaigns and to appeal to women.

DESIGN RATIONALE: The aim was to draw the customer into the store so a unit was designed that would be visually exciting. We didn't want to see the existing unit so we developed the stacked boxes. We wanted to emphasize that it was for women so we utilized mezzotints of each woman and enlarged them utilizing each women's 'Belief in fitness'. The shoes were displayed on top of the boxes so that the customer would need to walk all around the display. The colours were designed to complement store colours.

"L'Art de Vivre"

CLIENT: Flammarion 4, Paris, France

DESCRIPTION OF PRODUCT: Display unit; size 540 × 340 × 200mm to sell boxed sets of postcards and envelopes

DESIGNER: Flammarion 4, Paris, France

DATE OF COMPLETION: 1992

PLACE OF SALE: Booksellers

Product dispensers The structures in this chapter not only present and promote products, they are also specifically designed to allow us access. They contain quantities of a product and products rather than one perfectly presented specimen, and they keep them neatly arranged, are easy to examine, and most important of all, are easy to replenish. They extend the image of the product or the identity of the manufacturer. In some cases they indicate the price and the sales message, and they don't fall over!

But these are only the fundamentals of the brief. The designs also present their products in an isolated little environment that adds impact, prestige and clarity in the often chaotic surroundings of the shop floor.

Only
DRINK
Coca-Cola
REG. U.S. PAT. OFF.
IN BOTTLES
Serve Yourself
Delicious
and
Refreshing
COIN RETURN
BOTTLE OPENER

London Life

CLIENT: London Life, Bristol, UK

DESCRIPTION OF PRODUCT: Dispenser made from solid oak

DESIGNER: Aziz Cami & Stephen Gibbons, The Partners, London, UK

MAKER: Toby Winteringham

ILLUSTRATOR OR PHOTOGRAPHER: Brian McIntyre

DATE OF COMPLETION: 1988

TARGET MARKET: Wealthy consumer/financial product purchasers

PLACE OF SALE: Headquarters and regional offices of London Life

CLIENT'S BRIEF: Publication design is built around the way London Life does business, putting together a financial package for each individual client. All items of literature have to co-ordinate, since any combination could be appropriate. The Partners used the core idea of the nest egg, and devised witty variations to suit a Supersave Plan, a VIP Pension Scheme, or whatever.

DESIGN RATIONALE: The overall nest egg idea means that any combinations of product brochures can be assembled into a unified package for an individual client.

LONDON LIFE
VIP PENSION SCHEME
LONDON LIFE
REINVESTMENT BOND
LONDON LIFE
LINKED SAVINGS PLAN
LONDON LIFE
ANNUITIES
LONDON LIFE
LINKED INVESTMENT BOND
Established 1806

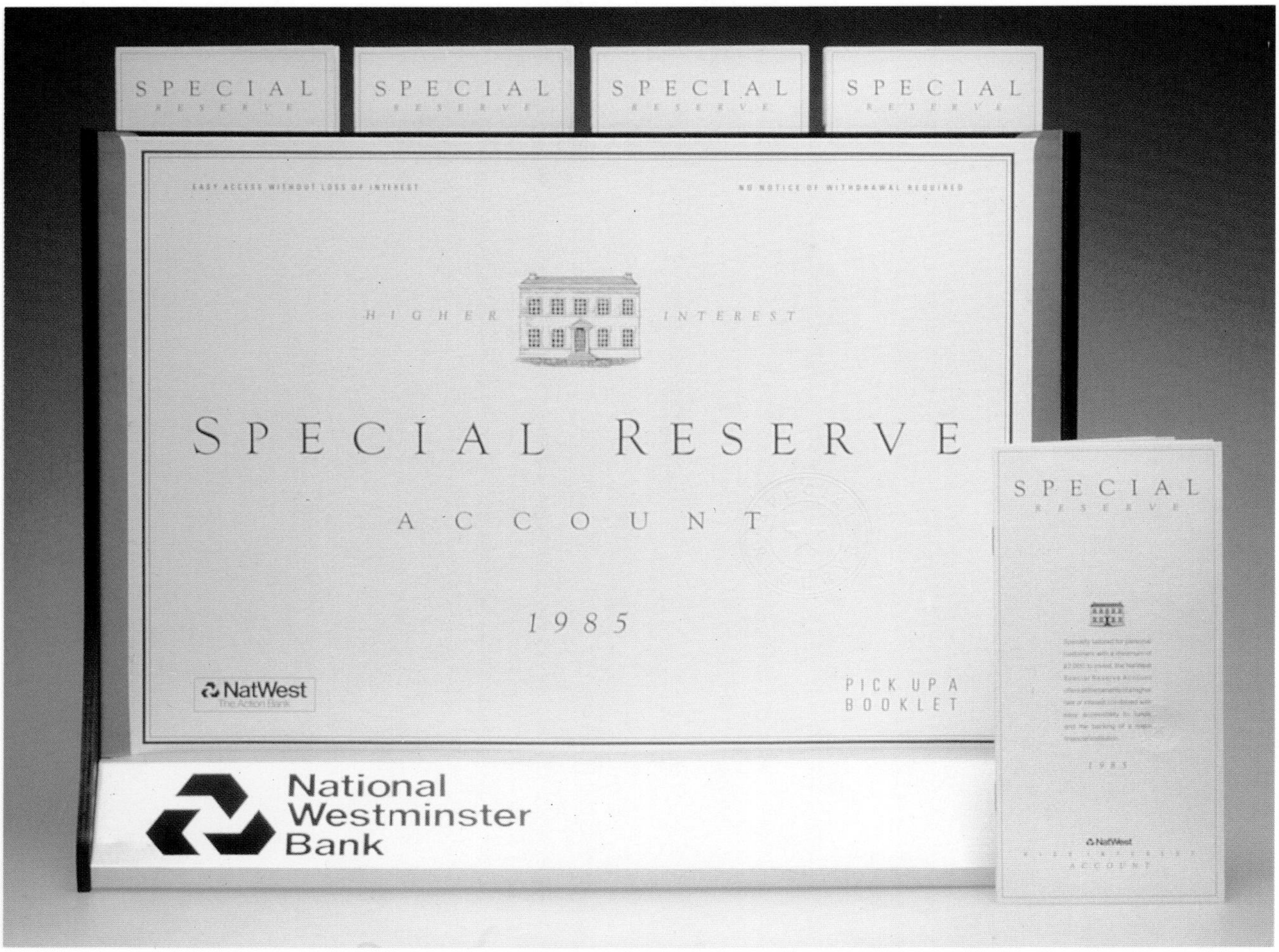

NatWest Students

CLIENT: NatWest Bank, London, UK

DESCRIPTION OF PRODUCT: Student leaflet and posters

DESIGNER: Michael Johnson, Smith & Milton, London, UK

PHOTOGRAPHERS: Martin Barrand, Trevor Key, Frank Farrelly, Inga Middleton

TARGET MARKET: 18+ new students on campus

PLACE OF SALE: In branches of NatWest and at Freshers' Fairs

Natwest Gold Plus

CLIENT: National Westminster Bank, London, UK

DESCRIPTION OF PRODUCT: Counter-top dispenser and brochure

DESIGNER: Minale Tattersfield & Partners Ltd, Richmond, Surrey, UK

DATE OF COMPLETION: 1986

TARGET MARKET: Gold Plus is NatWest's Premier financial service

PLACE OF SALE: Distributed from NatWest branches

CLIENT'S BRIEF: The brief from NatWest was to create a high-quality product with a select identity for this up-market target audience, in order to convey the considerable benefits package on offer from the NatWest Gold Plus service.

DESIGN RATIONALE: The design of the 'Gold Bar' which held the brochure reflected the value of the service.

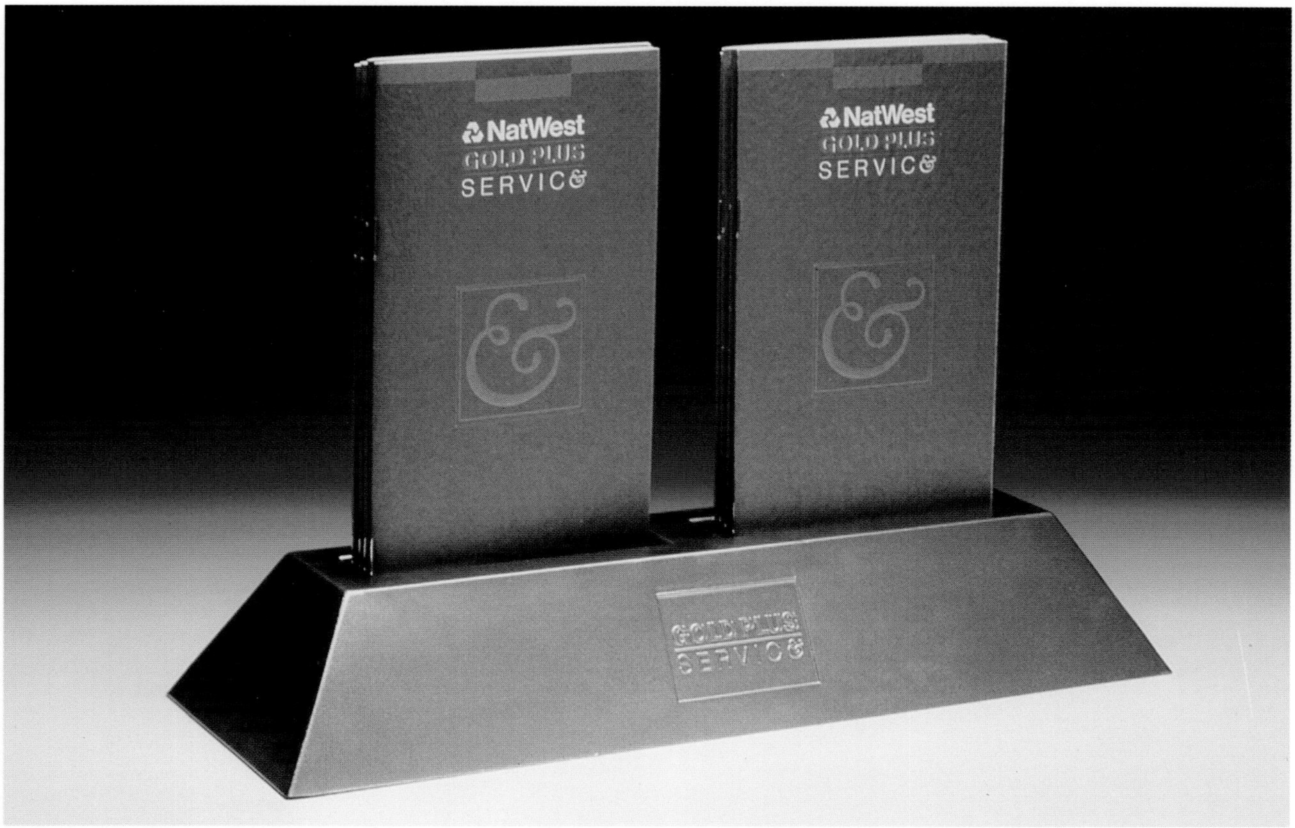

Sara Midda Promotion

CLIENT: Pan Books, London, UK

DESCRIPTION OF PRODUCT: Posters and dump bins for *Sketchbook from Southern France*

DATE OF COMPLETION: 1991

PLACE OF SALE: Bookshops

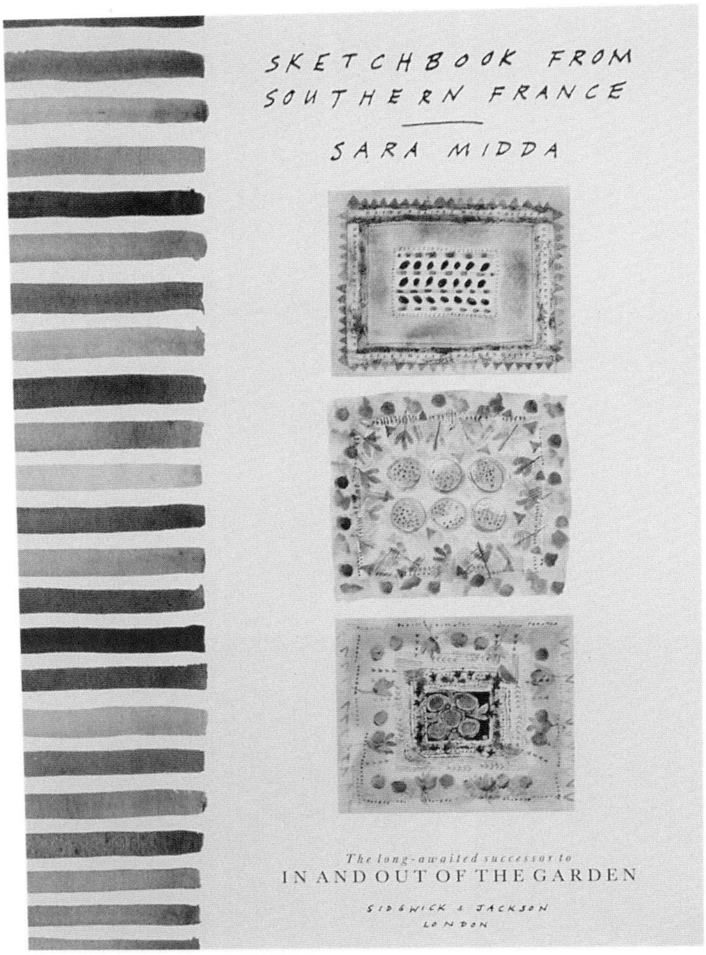

Michael Jackson; *The Legend Continues* (video)

CLIENT: Vestron Musicvideo, Stamford, Connecticut, USA

DESCRIPTION OF PRODUCT: Michael Jackson point-of-sale display and video-tape packaging. Corrugated cardboard: 4ft high × 1ft wide.

DESIGNER: Tim Nihoff and Scott Nash, Corey McPherson Nash, Watertown, MA, USA

ILLUSTRATOR OR PHOTOGRAPHER: Various

DATE OF COMPLETION: 1989

TARGET MARKET: Michael Jackson fans, young music lovers

PLACE OF SALE: Record stores and discount department stores

CLIENT'S BRIEF: To design the video-tape packaging and point-of-sale display.

DESIGN RATIONALE: The display is designed to work both as a table-top and free-standing display. The portion of the display that holds the tapes is designed so that when the stock of tapes are used or removed, the image of the packaging remains.

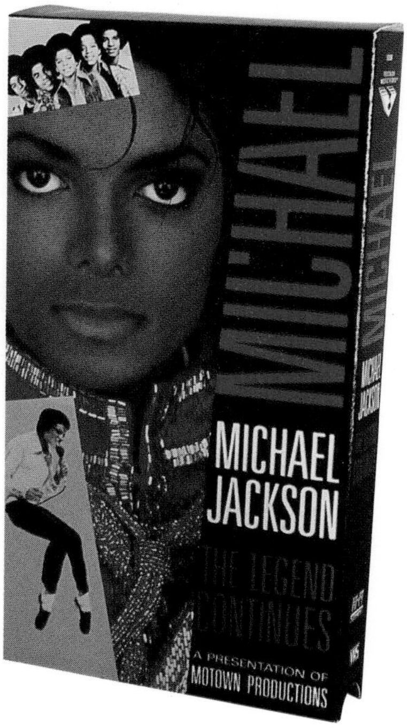

Trifari Department Store Jewelry Fixture

CLIENT: Trifari, Inc, New York, NY, USA

DESCRIPTION OF PRODUCT: Trifari Department Store Jewelry Fixture Programme

DESIGNER: Trans World Marketing, East Rutherford, NJ, USA

DATE OF COMPLETION: May 1990

TARGET MARKET: Females

PLACE OF SALE: Department stores

CLIENT'S BRIEF: To develop a unified department store refixturing programme, encompassing all aspects of Trifari's quality fashion jewelry line. To convey a sleek, contemporary image, yet offer superior functionality and space-efficient product presentation. To provide security, while affording easy customer access and shopability.

DESIGN RATIONALE: A contemporary colour scheme and dominant brand identification unify the entire programme, producing an elegant department store image. The displays illustrate innovative merchandizing, through use of a revolutionary wanding capability, as well as easy-to-operate pilfer-resistant merchanisms. The airy design of the displays enables Trifari sales personnel to have clear visibility of the entire jewelry counter area. Specially matched paper was used to create the marbelized look on tower headers and earring cards. The marbelized label on the surface of each tower hides slots which can be used for future earring bar placement.

Sarah Coventry Interactive Merchandizing Programme

CLIENT: R. N. Koch, Inc., Sarah Coventry Jewelry, Pawtucket, Rhode Island, USA

DESCRIPTION OF PRODUCT: Sarah Coventry Interactive Merchandizing Programme

DESIGNER: Trans World Marketing, East Rutherford, NJ, USA

DATE OF COMPLETION: February 1989

TARGET MARKET: Females

PLACE OF SALE: Mass merchandizers

CLIENT'S BRIEF: To revitalize the Sarah Coventry brand name and establish a high-quality image for a redesigned line of costume jewelry for the mass market.

DESIGN RATIONALE: To create a contemporary, eye-catching overall appearance that conveyed the department store image of Sarah Coventry Jewelry; and to provide space-efficient product merchandizing by use of rotating towers and individual earring panels in a relatively small footprint.

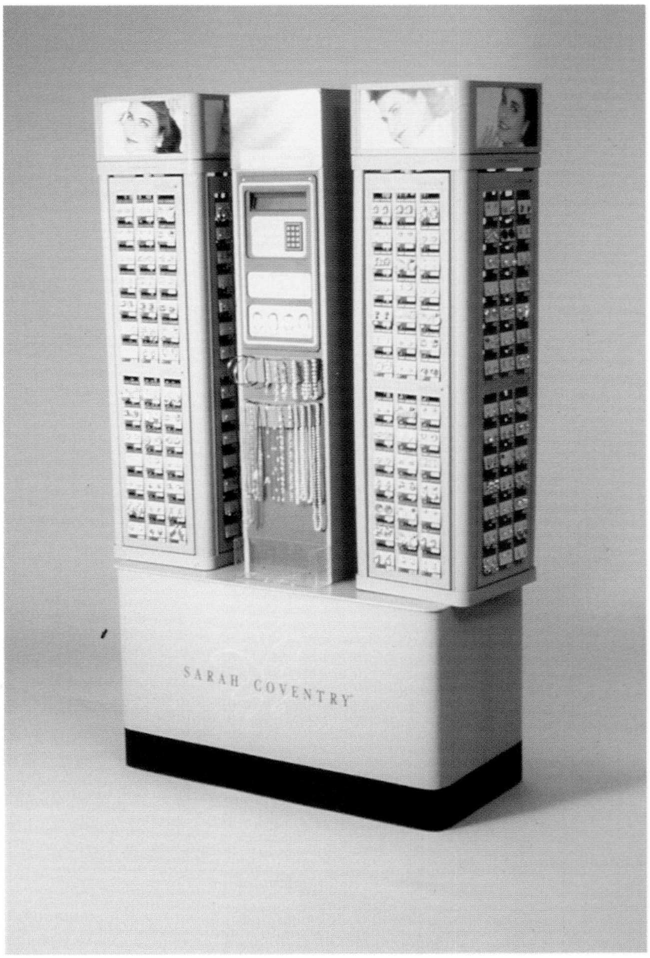

Rogé Cavailles

CLIENT: Procter and Gamble, Neuilly Sur Seine, France

DESCRIPTION OF PRODUCT: Lacquered wood; acrylic vacuum-forming; curved acrylic; size: height 1070mm; diameter 500mm

DESIGNER: Prisme, Suresnes, France

DATE OF COMPLETION: September 1991

TARGET MARKET: Everybody

PLACE OF SALE: Pharmacies and drugstores

CLIENT'S BRIEF: Since its creation in 1932, Rogé Cavailles soap has been recommended by both druggists and dermatologists. Although the products will be presented in a basket, the objective is to create a floor display with a special design to emphasize the quality, the purity and the legitimacy of Rogé Cavailles soaps.

DESIGN RATIONALE: The inspiration was 'Art Deco' style directly related to the creation of the product in 1932. The pure shape is in the form of a special and unique object. The high-quality materials reinforce this feeling. The display is designed to recall the bathroom and its environment: the use of transparent material evokes water, the use of a basin is to simulate the washbasin, so that the product is directly related to its function.

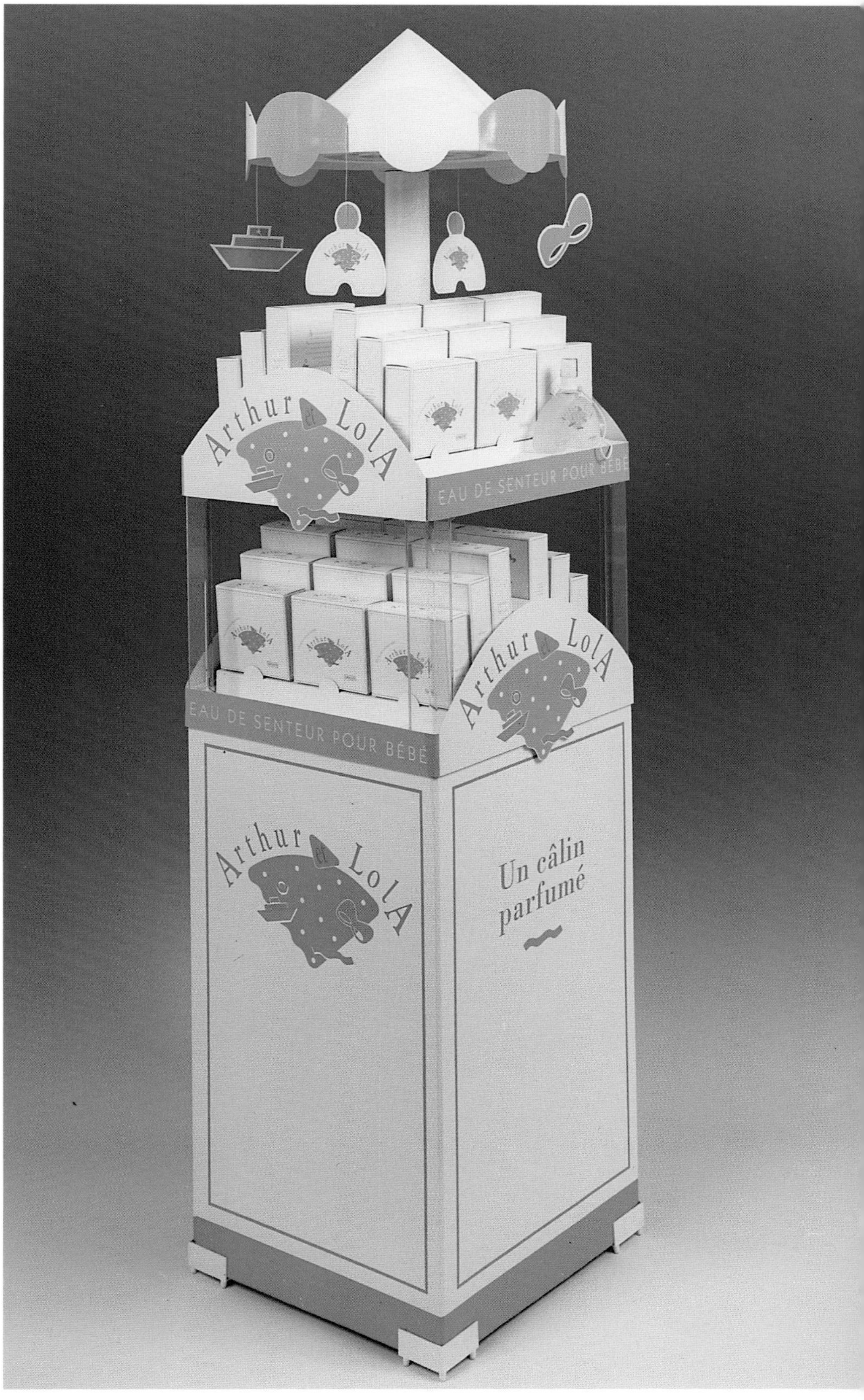

Arthur et Lola

CLIENT: Pharmhygiène, le Plessis Robinson, France
DESCRIPTION OF PRODUCT: Arthur et Lola floor-stand display
DESIGNER: Ateliers Reunis, Bagnolet, France
DATE OF COMPLETION: Winter 1991/92
PLACE OF SALE: Drugstores/pharmacies
CLIENT'S BRIEF: To create a floor-stand display for short-life direction for a new market area – baby perfume. The display needed to be accessible, light and compact.
DESIGN RATIONALE: The unit at the top of the display turns to attract attention; the display unit was cheap to produce and easy to move and clean, and it aroused the customer's curiosity – the aim of the point-of-sale material for this new product.

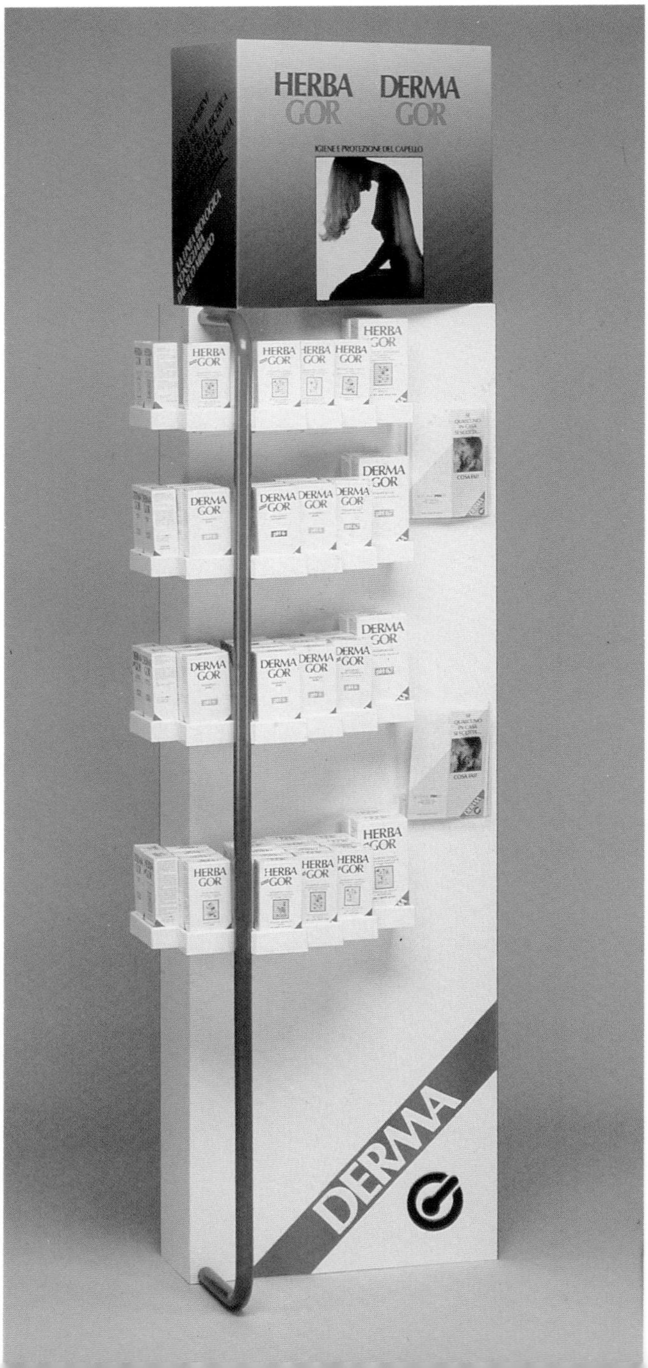

Derma

CLIENT: Biochimici P.S.N., Bologna, Italy

DESCRIPTION OF PRODUCT: Structure for products, sizes – small: 42 × 29 × 23cm; large: 190 × 50 × 45cm

DESIGNER: Studio Bonomi, Italy

ILLUSTRATOR OR PHOTOGRAPHER: Studio Bonomi

DATE OF COMPLETION: 1990–91

TARGET MARKET: High level

PLACE OF SALE: Pharmacies

CLIENT'S BRIEF: To create a floor-standing and counter-top display structure for a vast range of products. To create synthesized leaflet information for the customers.

DESIGN RATIONALE: To underline in both colours and materials the varied lines of different Derma products, and to make a suitable space for a product tester in the structure.

Studio Line Ravviva Ricci

CLIENT: Saipo L'Oreal, Torino, Italy

DESCRIPTION OF PRODUCT: Polystyrene carton: size 38 × 32 × 22in

DESIGNER: Studio Bonomi, Italy

ILLUSTRATOR OR PHOTOGRAPHER: Agenzia Pubblicitaria Della Oreal

DATE OF COMPLETION: 1990–1991

TARGET MARKET: Upper end youth market

PLACE OF SALE: Perfumeries

CLIENT'S BRIEF: To create a counter-top display which is both economical in terms of scale and takes the largest possible number of products; to unite the information leaflets in a single style.

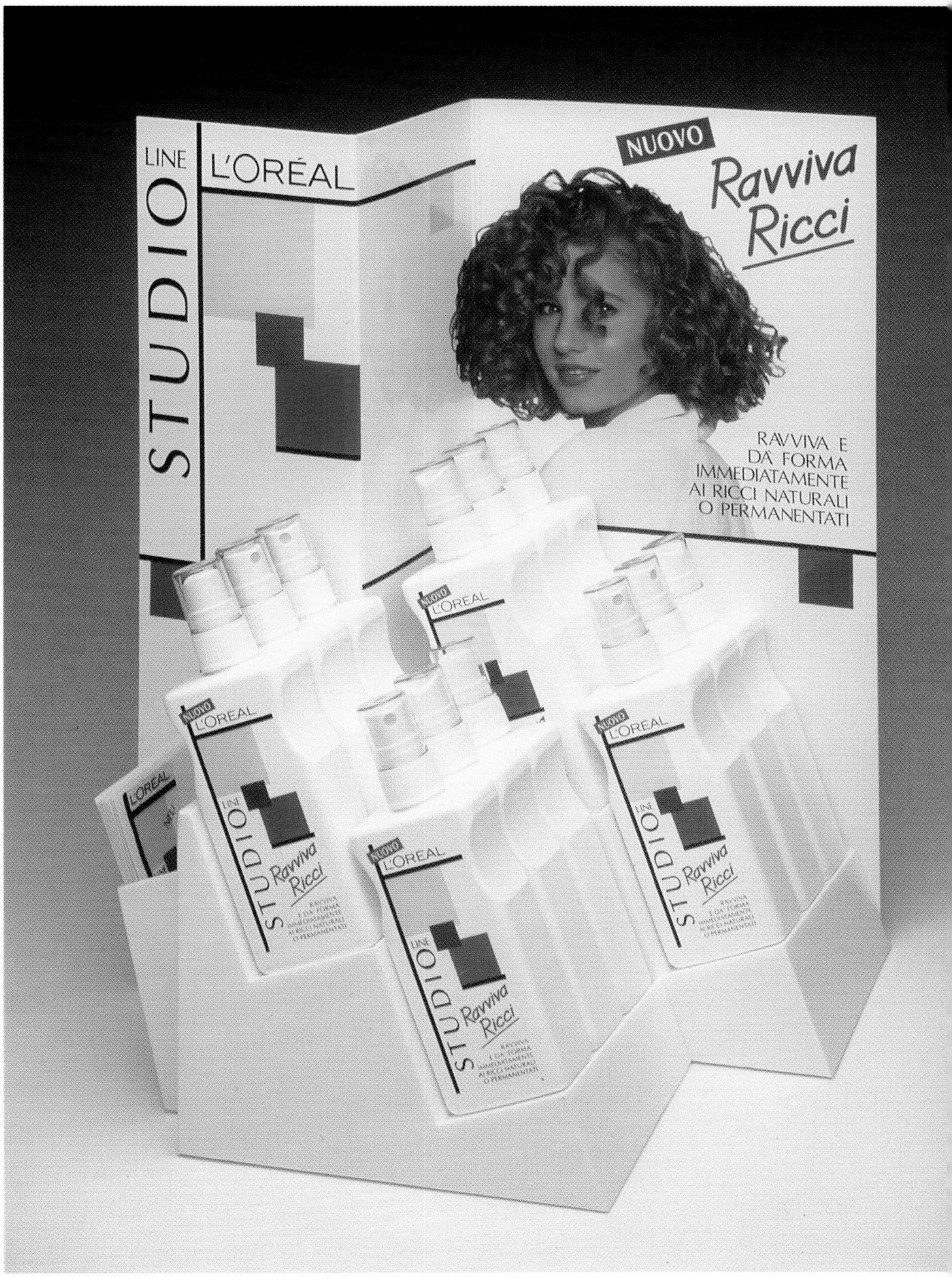

Coca-Cola
diet Coke
Coca-Cola CLASSIC
Coca-Cola CLASSIC
COCA-COLA CLASSIC
IT'S THE REAL THING
CAN'T BEAT THE FEELING
JUST FOR THE TASTE OF IT
I'D LIKE TO TEACH THE WORLD TO SING
I LIKE THE SPRITE IN YOU
SPRITE.
CHERRY COKE.
DIET COKE.
Enjoy Coca-Cola
Can't Beat The Real Thing.

Coca-Cola Jukebox Cooler

CLIENT: Coca Cola Co Ltd, New York, USA

DESCRIPTION OF PRODUCT: Constructed of glossy high-impact plastic with leak-proof drainage system with spigot

DESIGNER: Paul Flum Ideas Inc, New York, USA

DATE OF COMPLETION: Ongoing promotions

TARGET MARKET: To attract consumers to mass displays in supermarkets, hypermarkets etc.

PLACE OF SALE: Supermarkets, hypermarkets etc. (point-of-sale in retail chains)

DESIGN RATIONALE: The design is guaranteed to attract attention. It is a replica of a 1950s jukebox, featuring an insulated ice bin, glossy high-impact plastic construction and beautiful details. It is ideal as a dynamic dealer's leader, a great consumer premium, and as a perfect sampling unit.

Coca-Cola Nostalgia Cooler II

CLIENT: Coca Cola Co Ltd, New York, USA

DESCRIPTION OF PRODUCT: This cooler is a replica of a 1950's vending machine. It is constructed of glossy, high-impact plastic, detailed with authentic graphics and features a guaranteed drain system with spigot. Holds 99 12oz cans; 52 16oz bottles; 40 20oz bottles

DESIGNER: Paul Flum Ideas Inc, New York, USA

DATE OF COMPLETION: Ongoing promotions

TARGET MARKET: Consumers at supermarkets, hypermarkets

PLACE OF SALE: Supermarkets, hypermarkets (point-of-sale in retail chains)

DESIGN RATIONALE: The Nostalgia Cooler II was designed to guarantee placements in the highest quality, best traffic locations. It is also ideal as a dealer-loader and as a great consumer premium.

Seven-Up Giant Bottle

DESCRIPTION OF PRODUCT: Ice cabinet for 116 12oz cans; 72 16oz bottles; 58 20oz bottles

DESIGNER: Paul Flum Ideas Inc, New York, USA

DATE OF COMPLETION: Ongoing promotions

TARGET MARKET: Consumers in convenience stores, supermarkets, fast food outlets, gas mini-marts etc.

PLACE OF SALE: For point-of-sale displays in retail outlets

DESIGN RATIONALE: The giant bottle iceman is designed to replicate a Seven-Up bottle to attract consumers for increased single-serve sales. The unique bottle top end features openings in which consumers can reach through to obtain the products without taking off the lid.

Ultrabrite

CLIENT: Colgate Palmolive, Courbevoie, France

DESCRIPTION OF PRODUCT: Gondola or island display in double wall corrugated board printed in two colours flexo. Hand-mounted in 4 minutes. Transports in pallet size case, 800 × 600 × 150mm

DESIGNER: Stream-line, Paris, France

DATE OF COMPLETION: September 1990

TARGET MARKET: General public

PLACE OF SALE: Hypermarkets

CLIENT'S BRIEF: For Ultrabrites' fresh and vibrant image – a line extension around toothpaste into personal cosmetics – roll on, spray, shower gel, eau de toilette. All products to be displayed at the same time in a single easy-to-construct display. Ultrabrite has a strong, monolithic, clean, fresh image, to be reflected in an impressive, imposing design. Must hold over 250kg (1/4 tonne).

DESIGN RATIONALE: The style – imposing, impressive, tall and dark – reflects Ultrabrite's brand identity. Vertical graphics on corner supports enhance the effect. Solid and inventive board engineering creates a stable structure that is easy to put up *in situ* and easy to fill and display. One pallet holds all products and the display mounting in the flat.

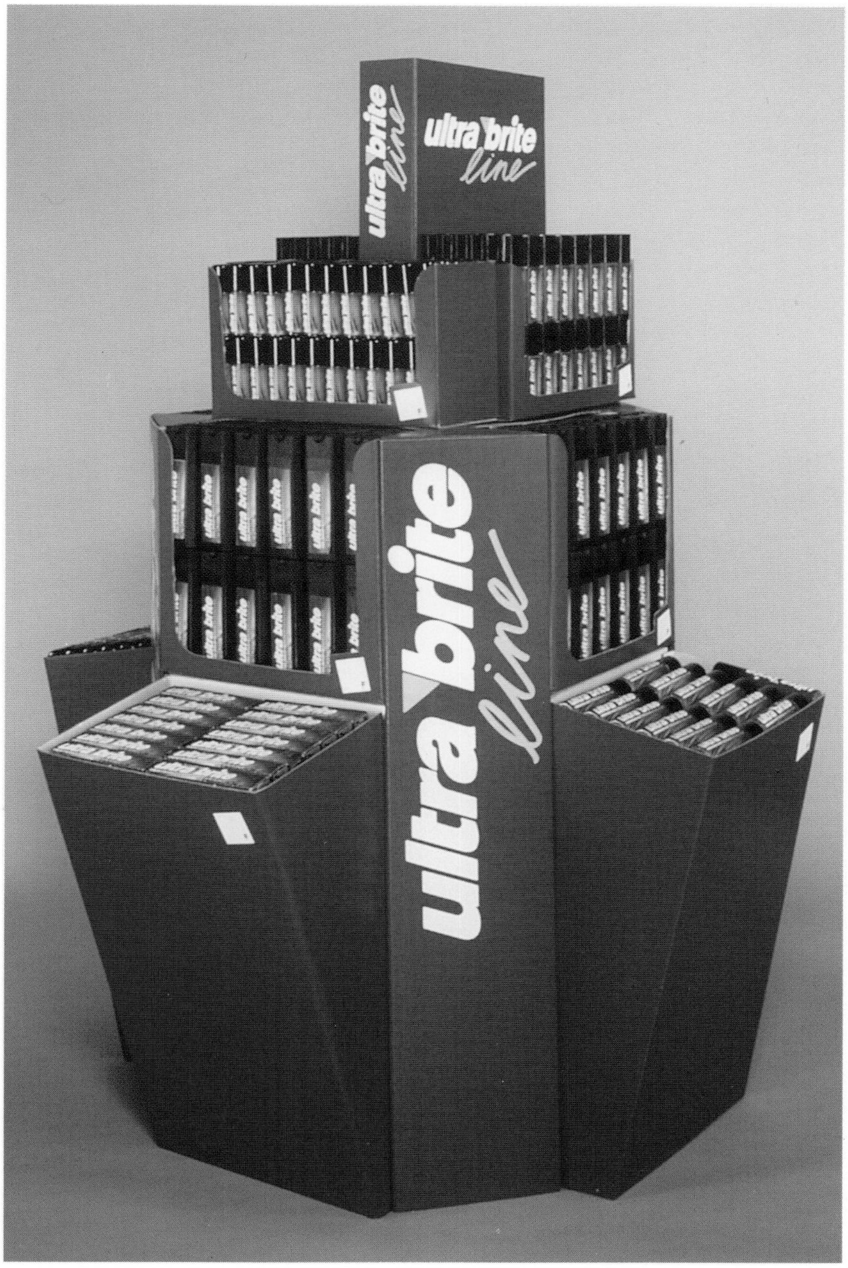

L.A. Looks Cosmetic Kit

CLIENT: Los Angeles Research Packaging, Los Angeles, California, USA

DESCRIPTION OF PRODUCT: Make-up kits containing eye shadows and blushers. One dozen kits in a point-of-sale display.

DESIGNER: Mamoru Shimokochi, Anne Reeves, Tracy McGoldrick, Shimokochi/Reeves Design, Los Angeles, California, USA

DATE OF COMPLETION: Christmas 1991

TARGET MARKET: 13–15 age group

PLACE OF SALE: Mass merchandise and drug stores in the USA

CLIENT'S BRIEF: Due to the success of the LA Looks hair styling line, it was decided to extend the brand image to a Cosmetic Kit targeted at the young teens. The Cosmetic Kit package and point-of-sale had to reflect the same fun, Southern California attitude and project the quality and feeling of the LA Looks styling line – appealing to those who aspire to the youthful LA image. The purchase was seasonal, planned for the Christmas and back-to-school market.

DESIGN RATIONALE: The Cosmetic kit and point-of-sale captures the fun and excitement of the original LA Looks styling line. A unique identity was created for the Cosmetic Kit through the use of vibrant colour and graphic elements, projecting a gift-like quality.

A Gift of a Tree

CLIENT: Earth Plan, Sherman Oaks, California, USA

DESCRIPTION OF PRODUCT: A gift certificate greeting card for a tree-planting kit and display box, printed on recycled paper

DESIGNER: Mamoru Shimokochi, Anne Reeves, Shimokochi/Reeves Design, Los Angeles, California, USA

DATE OF COMPLETION: 1991

TARGET MARKET: Environmentally conscious consumers and the general public

PLACE OF SALE: Throughout the USA

CLIENT'S BRIEF: A new and unique product concept. A gift certificate greetings card which helps the environment. Each certificate represents the planting of a tree. The objective: to develop a strong point-of-sale item to display the earth-sensitive greetings cards and reflect trees and the environment.

DESIGN RATIONALE: The design reflects the uniqueness of the gift certificate concept and the concern for the environment. The use of recycled paper, and fine detailed line drawings of trees and birds, further strengthen the overall message and sensitivity to the cause.

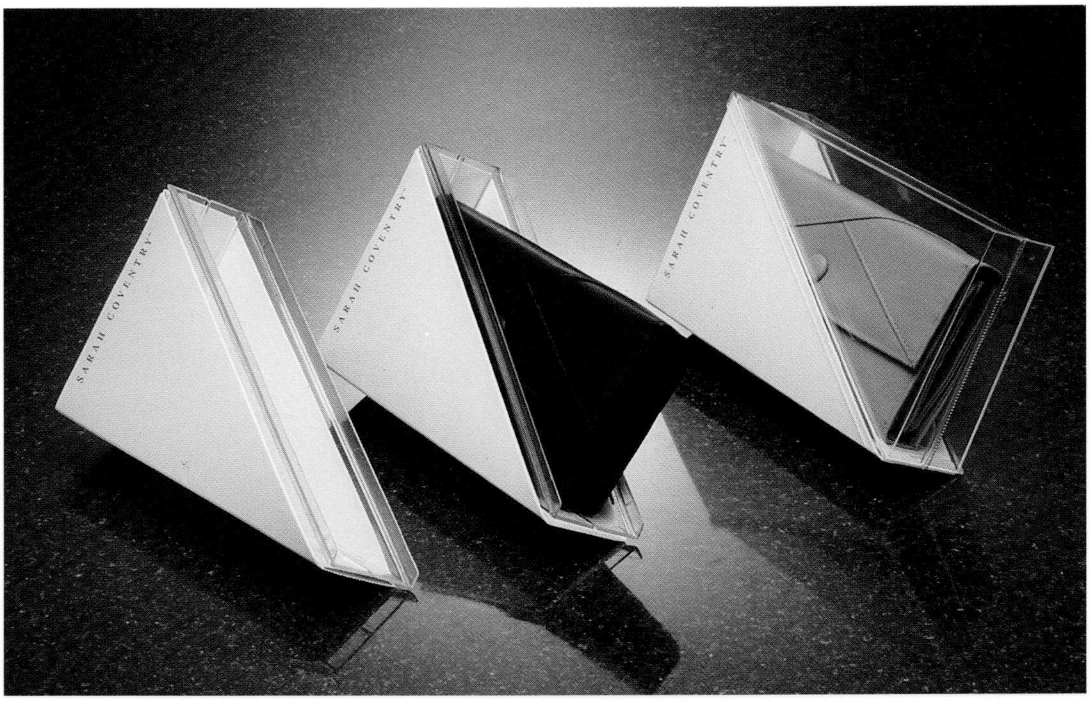

Sarah Coventry Small Leather Goods

CLIENT: RGA, New York, NY, USA

DESCRIPTION OF PRODUCT: Women's leather purses, wallets; 2 sizes only

DESIGNER: Barry Berger, Art Martin, Tom Stoeckle, Heidi Sklenar, Barry David Berger + Associates, Inc., New York, NY, USA

ILLUSTRATOR OR PHOTOGRAPHER: Julian Kaiser

DATE OF COMPLETION: 1990

TARGET MARKET: Mass merchandizers

PLACE OF SALE: K-Mart, Walmart, Sears

CLIENT'S BRIEF: To develop a 100% recyclable gift package that displays its contents (women's wallets, cheque books) so that all of the product's details are seen/touched easily; to develop a display that holds two each of 60 styles and induces the retailer to use the display.

DESIGN RATIONALE: The gift package provides full product access. Two sizes are available. The display fixture's tray is open to eliminate trash and angles downward so that it "housekeeps" itself by using centrifugal force to guarantee that all packages are positioned forward. The retailer is more likely to use the display, which increases the rate of sales.

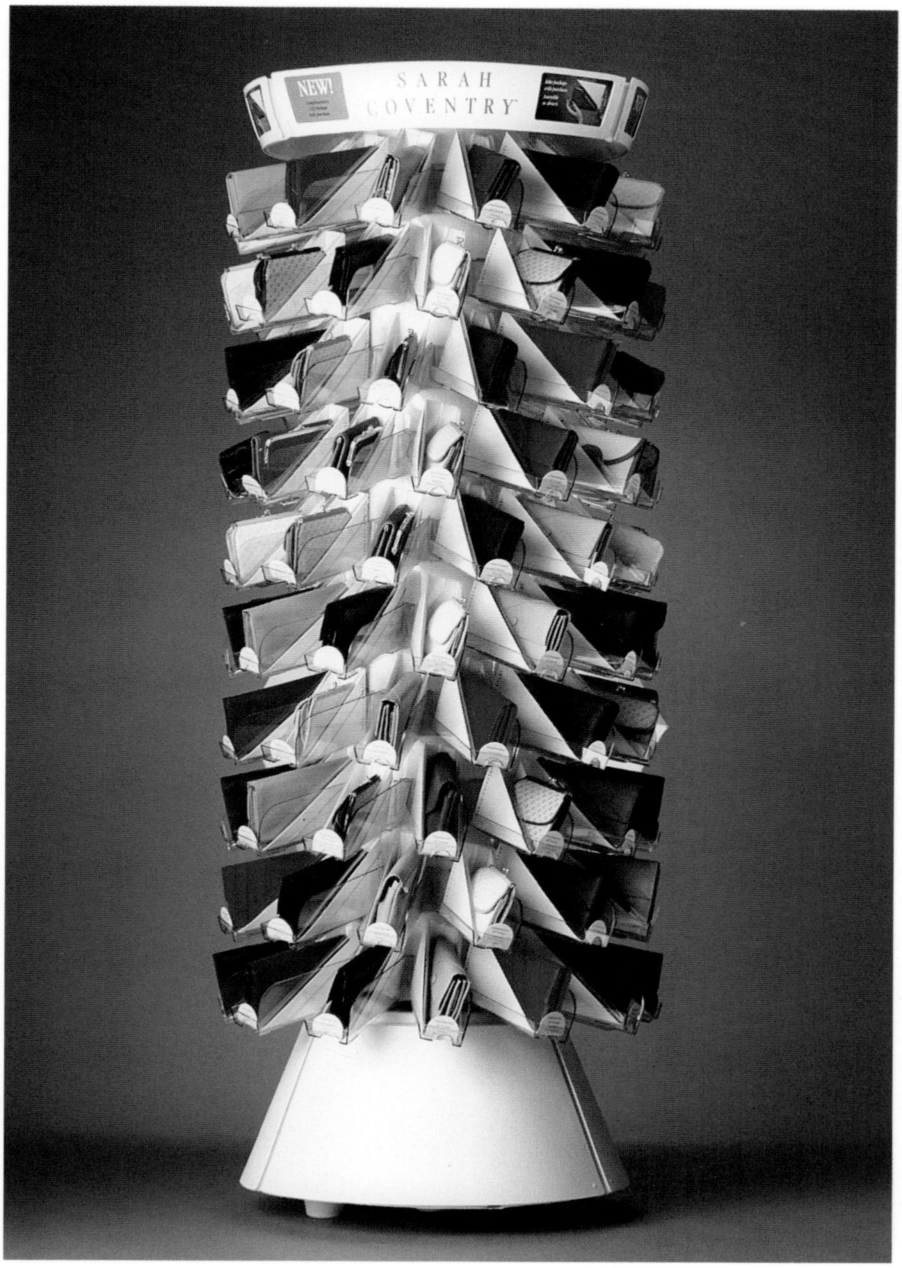
SARAH
COVENTRY
NEW!

11, RUE EUGENE LOZES
CACHOU
LAJAUNIE
PHARMACIEN
TOULOUSE
FRANCE

Displays Cachou Lajaunie

CLIENT: Cachou Lajaunie, Toulouse, France

DESCRIPTION OF PRODUCT: Both the displays are made out of a backing of formed and injected polystyrene (to obtain a very low fabrication cost)

DESIGNER: RS Creation, Montreuil, France

DATE OF COMPLETION: Display 1 1986; Display 2 1989

TARGET MARKET: Any

PLACE OF SALE: Tobacco shops, service stations, drugstores.

CLIENT'S BRIEF: The goal was to create a stocking display that was as small as possible, manufactured in very large numbers (40,000 samples), valourizing the product and carrying an image which was both 'going back to the past' and 'in fashion' for this revived product.

DESIGN RATIONALE: Through its design the first project is reminiscent of the very old radios, the Wurlitzer juke boxes and the old French milestone. In the header card, the facing of an oversized tin was integrated. The design is voluntarily 'back to the past'.

The second project is a renewal of the first but with two new factors: an optimal visualization of the product and the integration of a new flavour of the product, which explains the double signature.

City

CLIENT: Waterman SA, Paris, France

DESCRIPTION OF PRODUCT: One piece injection-moulded display with engraving and silkscreen print. Mould is a simple two-piece without sliders.

DESIGNER: Stream-line, Paris, France

DATE OF COMPLETION: September 1989

TARGET MARKET: Students and schoolchildren

PLACE OF SALE: All stationers, bookshops, kiosks etc.

CLIENT'S BRIEF: For a new range of pens aimed at schoolchildren and students, Waterman were looking for a counter display that set off the products on a fashionable background. The display had to be economic, low in tooling costs, filled in the factory and immediately usable by retailers.

DESIGN RATIONALE: Stream-line invented a 'Big City' theme, with a flashing neon and skyscraper background, to set off this fashionable and colourful pen. The pens are suspended by an innovative moulding detail, and soar in crossed banks into the air. The front panel carries the big city in relief.

Timex Watches

CLIENT: Timex, Waterbury, Connecticut, USA

DESCRIPTION OF PRODUCT: Showcase

DESIGNER: Barry David Berger & Associates Inc, New York, USA

CLIENT'S BRIEF: It was the first package to re-design in nine years. It had to be among first gift packages under Christmas tree to be opened; it had to have high-tech package styling to overcome a stodgy product image.

DESIGN RATIONALE: The main elements of the design rationale were: it had to be easy to gift wrap; it had to have minimum left-to-right dimension; it had to have maximum internal volume. The display graphics had to be keyed to the consumer's lifestyle and to the product's design. The point-of-sale fixture had to appear like a museum showcase and to light every product evenly and equally.

Visolaire

CLIENT: Dr van der Hoog, Netherlands

DESCRIPTION OF PRODUCT: Skin-care cosmetics

DESIGNER: Stadium Design BV, Hillegom, Netherlands

DATE OF COMPLETION: Spring 1991

TARGET MARKET: Upper level purchasers of cosmetics

Tops

CLIENT: Bryant & May Ltd, High Wycombe, Bucks, UK
DESCRIPTION OF PRODUCT: Matches
DESIGNER: Michael Sheridan & Co Ltd, 40 Nelson St, Leicester, UK
DATE OF COMPLETION: 1989
TARGET MARKET: Smokers, middle market, 16–45 years
PLACE OF SALE: Confectioners, tobacconists and newsagents
CLIENT'S BRIEF: To display the product and get the maximum stock-holding in retail outlets where space is at a premium. A permanent merchanizer for use in CTNs and pubs. The matches are positioned as a fashion accessory for smokers and command a premium price.
DESIGN RATIONALE: High-volume manufacture and quality of presentation resulted in an injection-moulded gravity-feed merchandizer/dispenser with good product visibility. Vertical stock-holding ensures high-stockholding-to-space occupancy. Base is removable for wall positioning as well as standard counter or shelf positioning.

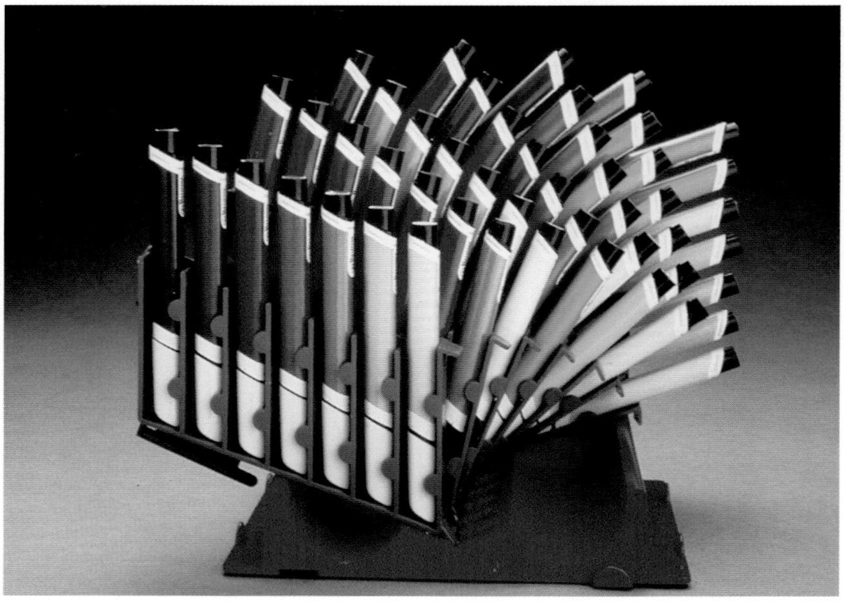

Letraset

CLIENT: Letraset, Paramus, New Jersey, USA

DESCRIPTION OF PRODUCT: Professional zylon-base markers

DESIGNER: Barry David Berger & Associates, Inc, New York, USA

ILLUSTRATOR OR PHOTOGRAPHER: Barry David Berger & Associates, Inc

PLACE OF SALE: Art materials retailers, design professionals

CLIENT'S BRIEF: To increase the client's market share by: providing the most effective point-of-sale fixtures to retailers whose clients purchase markers through visits to retail art material stores; providing the most flexible, effective marker organizer for retailers to give or sell to clients who purchase markers by phone or fax orders. To provide both the desk-top organizer and the modular point-of-sale fixture by using as many identical parts as possible, to reduce capital investment.

DESIGN RATIONALE: Letraset's markers' colours are keyed to the Pantone colour matching system. Their labels are carefully printed to match their ink colours. The left/right priority marker cassette permits extreme close-packing while allowing the shopper to 'open' the display fixture at any location, and the front/back hinge allows easy access to pre-selected palettes.

Pantone Color Markers
by Letraset
Letraset

Pantone Color Markers
by Letraset
Letraset

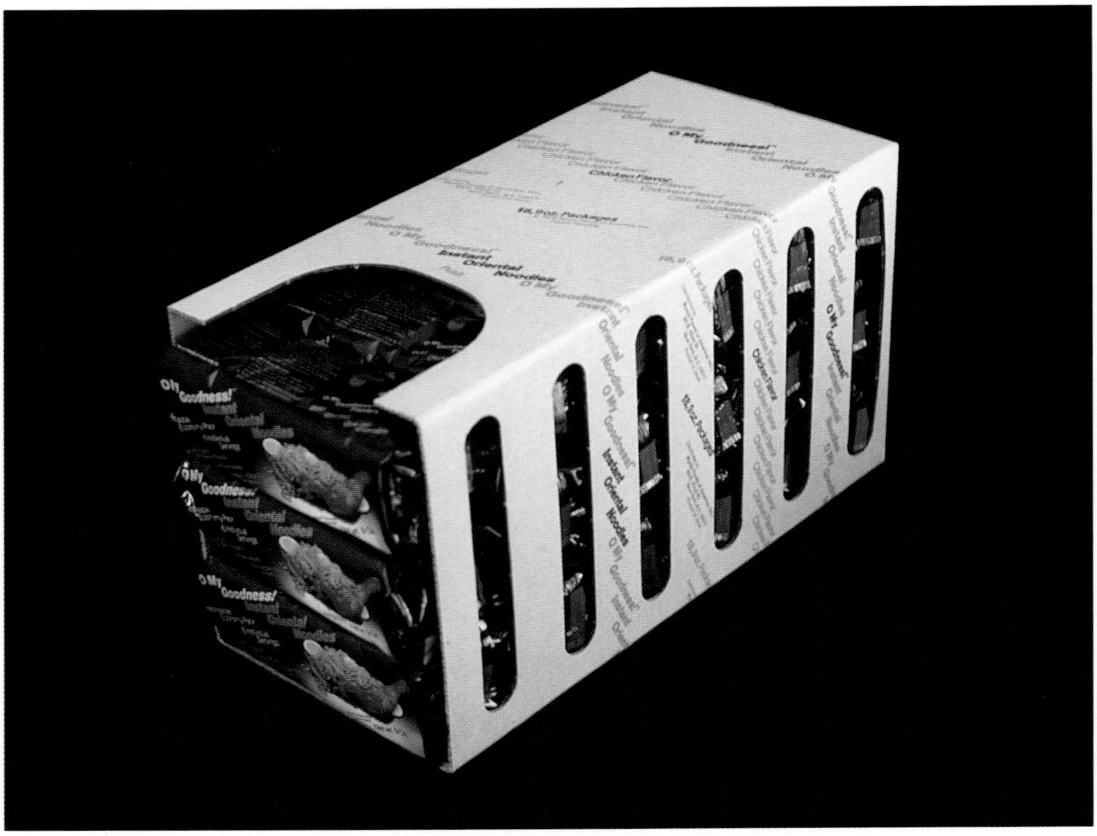

Oh My Goodness (instant oriental noodle packaging)

CLIENT: Myojo Foods of America, Inc, New York, USA

DESCRIPTION OF PRODUCT: Japanese eggless ramen in six flavours

DESIGNER: Robert P. Gersin Assoc. Inc, New York, USA

DATE OF COMPLETION: 1979

TARGET MARKET: American consumers through grocery stores, supermarkets and convenience stores

PLACE OF SALE: As above

CLIENT'S BRIEF: To develop appropriate positioning and package to introduce a ramen product manufactured in Japan to the American market . It had to appeal to consumers who view a noodle dish as an accompaniment to a main dish or as a snack. It also had to create a distinctive system of packages that would compete on the grocers' shelf with a variety of other similar products and allow for line extension.

DESIGN RATIONALE: The soft packs are difficult for the retailer to display neatly. The shipper display carton allowed the grocer to get at die-cut sections for pricing (without removing them) and neatly displayed the product. The packages remain fresh-looking for the consumer.

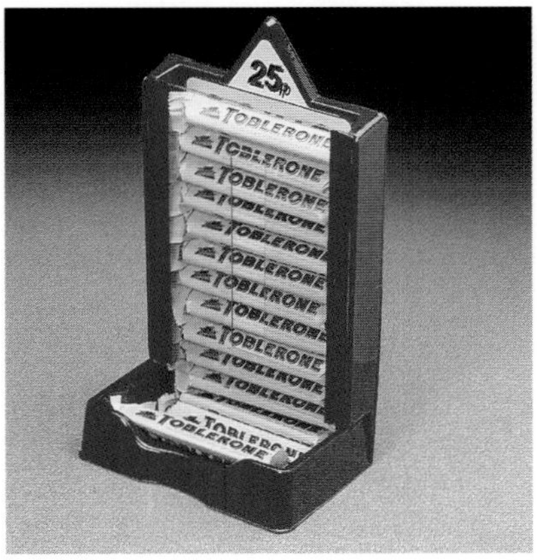

Toblerone

CLIENT: Suchard Ltd, Cheltenham, Glos., UK

DESCRIPTION OF PRODUCT: Counter display unit for Toblerone 35g bars. Vac-formed, coloured PVC and acetate print, 12in high

DESIGNER: J Schwartz, Cheltenham, Glos., UK

ILLUSTRATOR OR PHOTOGRAPHER: Link Marketing Design

DATE OF COMPLETION: January 1992

TARGET MARKET: Male and female consumers of Toblerone, 20–35 years old

PLACE OF SALE: Specifically designed to increase display within the newsagent, tobacconist and confectioners' stores

CLIENT'S BRIEF: To design a 'disposable' display unit for Toblerone that would secure space for the brand near the prime cash register area. The unit would probably be discarded after two months by the retailer and therefore the increased sales generated by the display would have to cover the units costs within this period.

DESIGN RATIONALE: Space is very precious for the retailer and therefore the unit would only be used if it took up as little surface area as possible. By putting the stock 'up in the air' a box of bars can be stored using only a fraction of the surface area. The bars create the display's branding.

SYSTEMA SEBASTIAN
HI ENERGY HOLD
HOLD AND MOLD
MOISTURE SHAMPOO
FORMULATING CREME
CREMA RE-SIZING CREME
THE ELEMENTS OF DESIGN

Systema Hair Care

CLIENT: Sebastian, Woodland Hills, California, USA

DESCRIPTION OF PRODUCT: Systema point-of-sale display. Injection-moulded to display the Systema Hair Care Line. The display measures 18in × 17in × 17in approximately.

DESIGNER: Stuart Karten Design, Marina del Rey, California, USA

ILLUSTRATOR OR PHOTOGRAPHER: Domenic Marsden

DATE OF COMPLETION: 1988

TARGET MARKET: Females aged 15–30

PLACE OF SALE: Professional hair salons

CLIENT'S BRIEF: To create an interesting, eye-catching counter display to support two to three examples of each product.

DESIGN RATIONALE: Systema, The Elements of Design, was the client's name for the product line. The tag line 'Elements of Design' was capitalized on by constructing the display from the three-dimensional elements of design: the cone and cube and sphere. These elements were floated on an organic form and bridged with shelves to support the product. The dynamics of all these elements created a striking overall form that attracted the customer to the display.

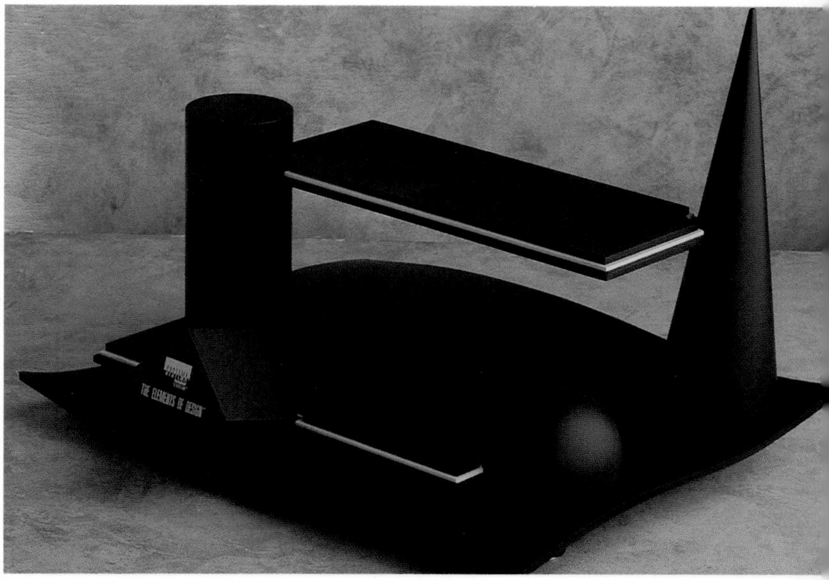

Coordinated schemes Design companies and marketing departments, once they have designed a new product, will look for ways of extending the imagery to broaden its exposure and increase its impact. In a bank or a building society, leaflets and showcards, dispensers, posters and window graphics can all be designed to coordinate. The image of a new or redesigned product can be extended to include dumpbins and signage. A new musical or pop event will have a continuity of graphics – from the posters and advertising to the programmes and the T-shirts of its ushers and backstage crew.

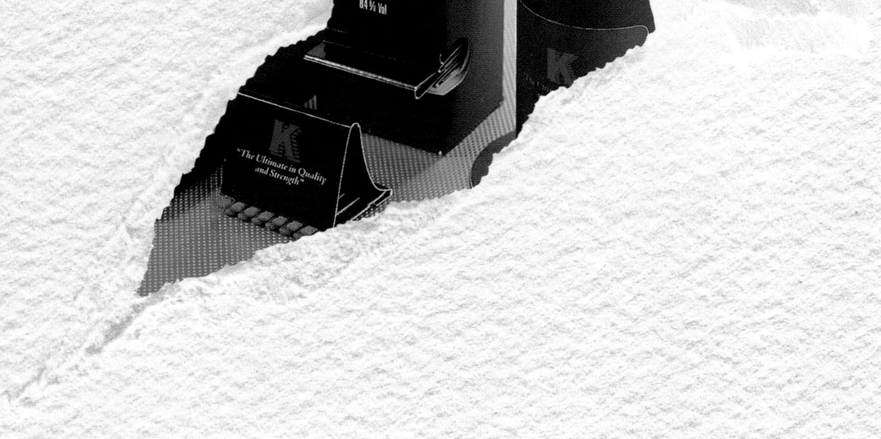

MENS C
ECO
illac
AGE
ARDWEAR Co
Finer!

Camper Brutus

CLIENT: Camper-Coflusa, Mallorca, Spain
DESCRIPTION OF PRODUCT: Display for a shoe style
DESIGNER: Carlos Rolando, CR Communication & Design Services, Barcelona, Spain
DATE OF COMPLETION: 1988
TARGET MARKET: People of any age
PLACE OF SALE: Camper shops all over Spain
CLIENT'S BRIEF: Camper communication philosophy consists in never showing the shoes in photographs, but using an eclectic, sometimes naïve, sometimes intellectual approach, through illustration or methaphor, thus creating a peculiar communication style built on many different graphic forms.
DESIGN RATIONALE: In the case of this product, the creative concept was based on creating a brand identity for this kind of working shoes. By using strong graphics, the product is given a more trendy image.

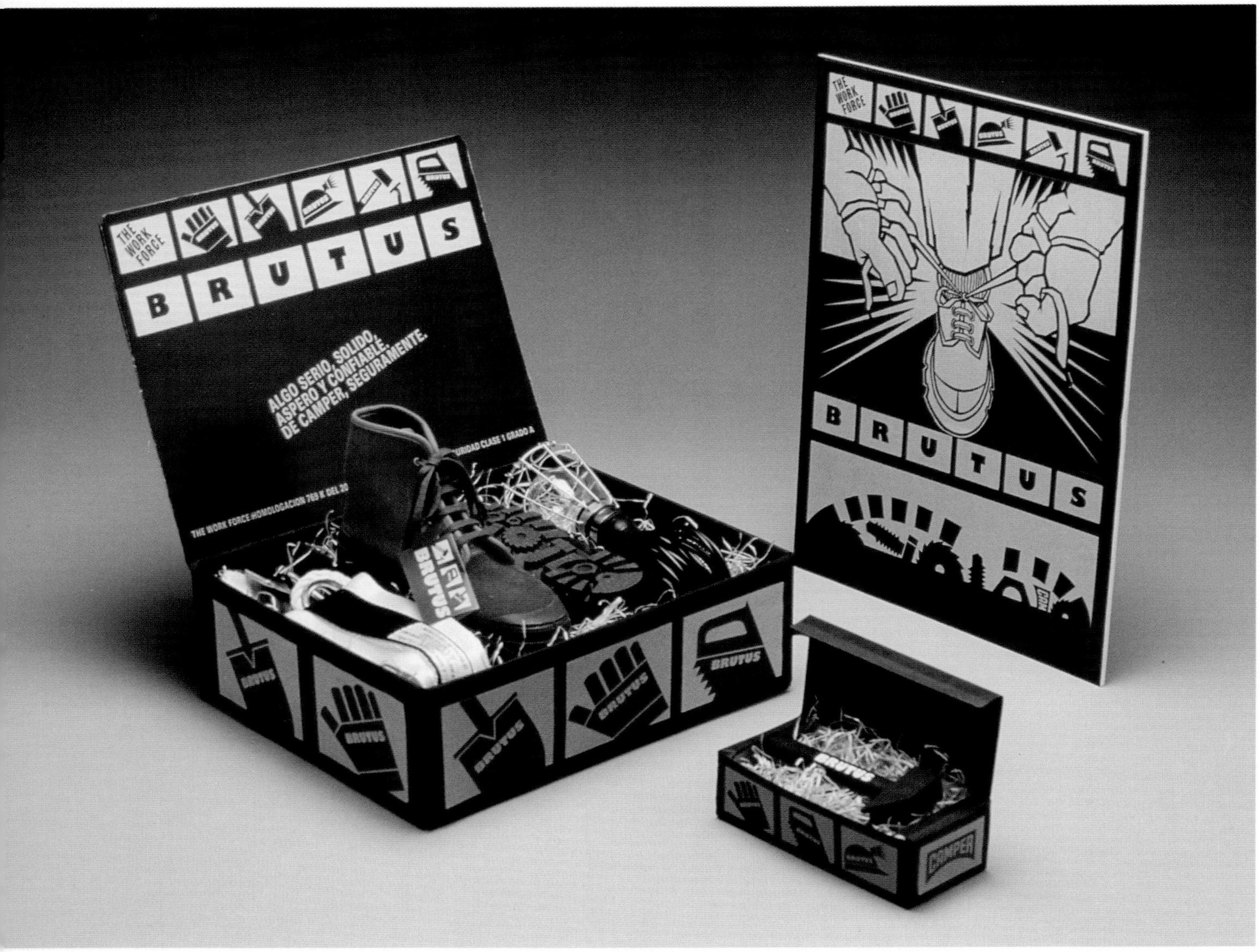

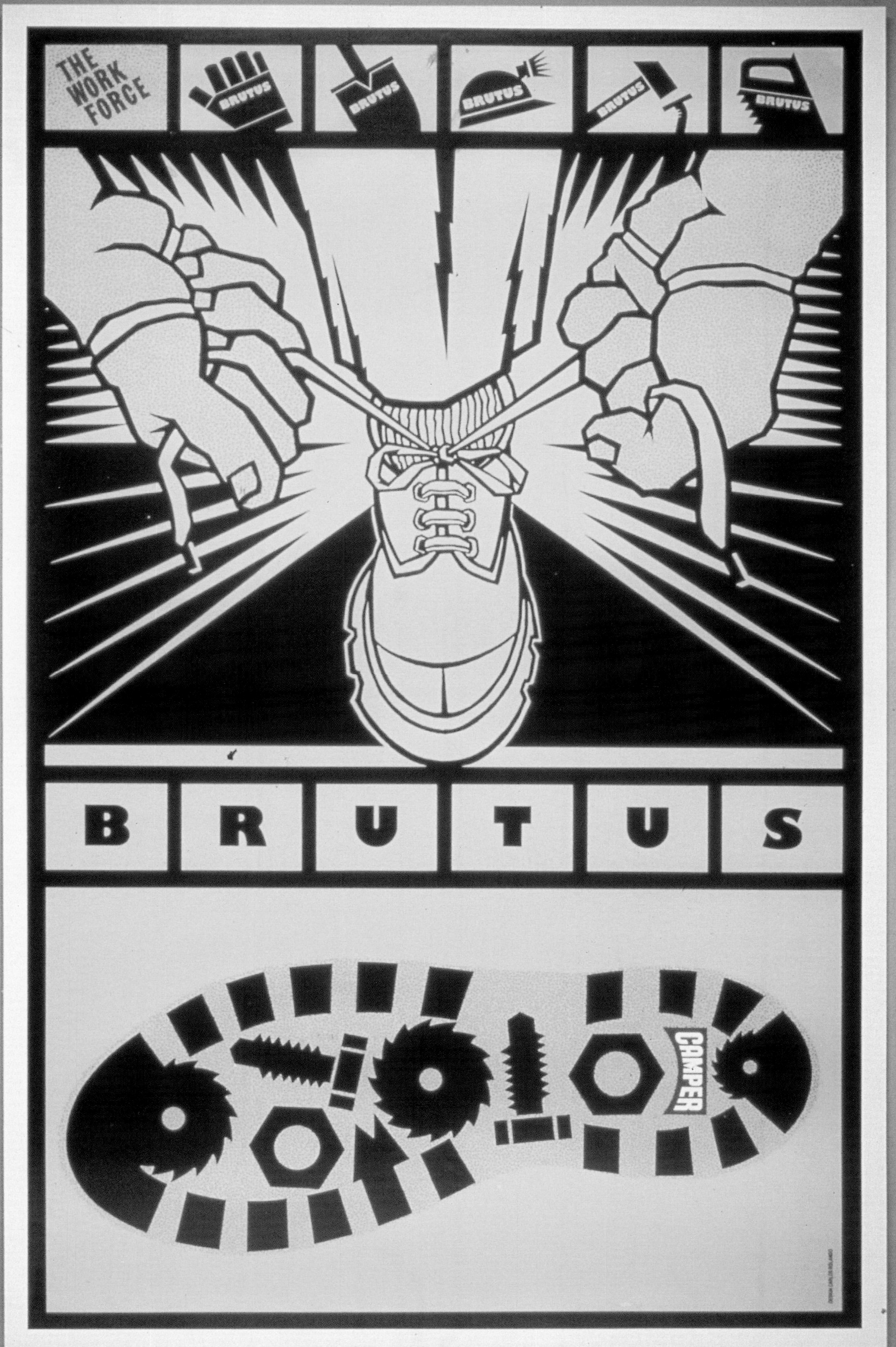
THE WORK FORCE
BRUTUS
BRUTUS
BRUTUS
BRUTUS
BRUTUS
B R U T U S
CAMPER

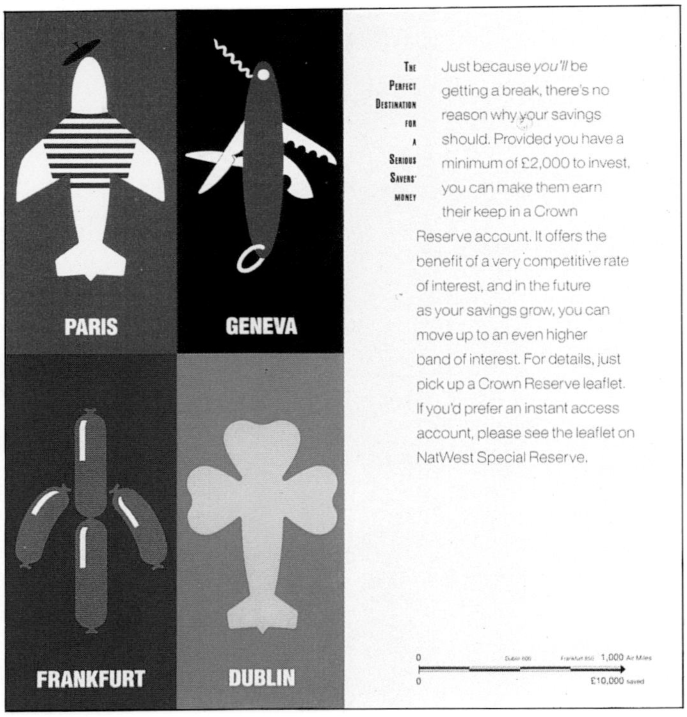

Airmiles

CLIENT: Natwest Bank, London, UK

DESCRIPTION OF PRODUCT: Point-of-sale posters and leaflets

DESIGNER: Michael Johnson, Smith & Milton, London, UK

ILLUSTRATOR: Michael Johnson, Janice Davison

TARGET MARKET: Natwest Airmiles collectors/potential collectors

PLACE OF SALE: In branches

CLIENT'S BRIEF: To encourage subscriptions to airmiles schemes by *saving* money, rather than spending. For every £10 saved, subscribers received one airmile.

DESIGN RATIONALE: "Save with us, fly free" was a working copyline that became real when we took a mile of air and showed it in the plane shape. We could then take the symbol and change it and play a few humorous games to help people see where they could fly to.

Dillons

CLIENT: Pearce Retailing Ltd, Birmingham, UK

DESIGNER: Stocks Taylor Benson Ltd, Leics, UK

ILLUSTRATOR OR PHOTOGRAPHER: Copyright-Free Images

DATE OF COMPLETION: February 1990

TARGET MARKET: ABC male/female equal bias, 25–60 years

PLACE OF SALE: Dillons, Athena Bookstores (approximately 100 outlets)

CLIENT'S BRIEF: To create an Easter visual identity appropriate to the religious timing without resorting directly to crucifixion images.

DESIGN RATIONALE: The use of architectural style illustrations of churches hit the right balance between religion and seriousness, but was still attractive and sophisticated.

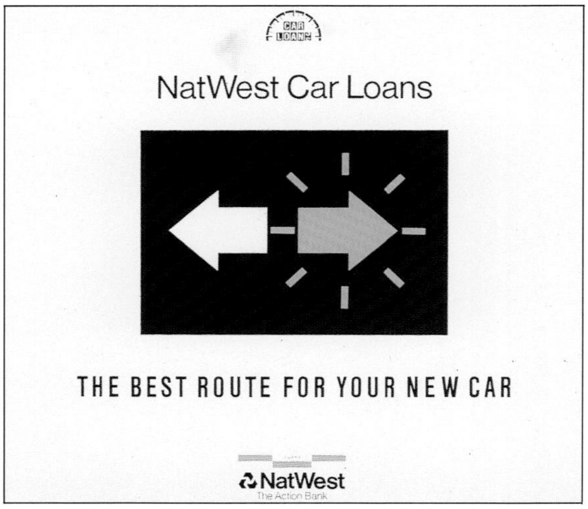
NatWest Car Loans
THE BEST ROUTE FOR YOUR NEW CAR
NatWest
The Action Bank

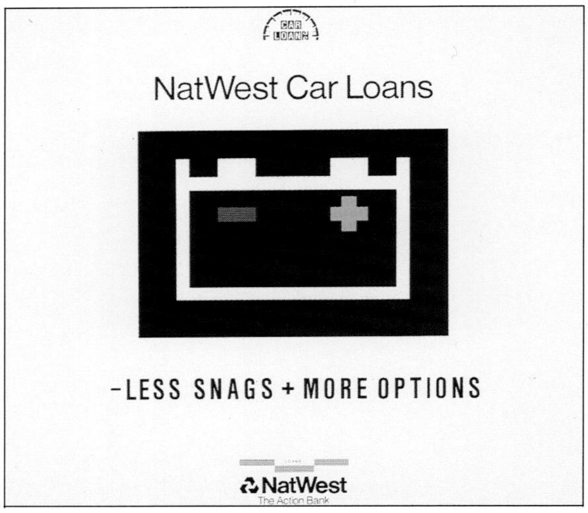
NatWest Car Loans
-LESS SNAGS + MORE OPTIONS
NatWest
The Action Bank

NatWest Car Loans
SMOOTH YOUR TRANSACTIONS
NatWest

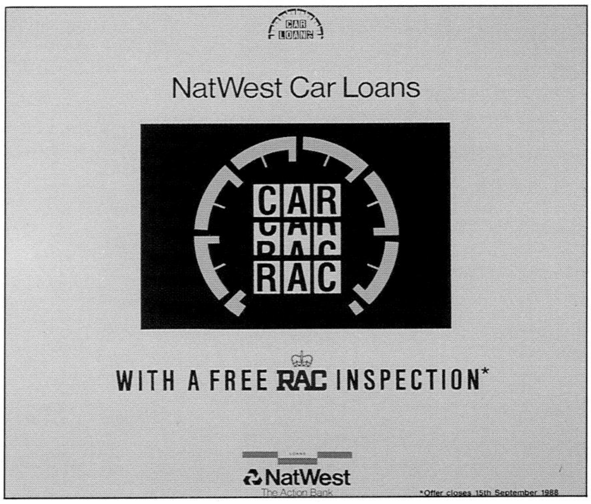
NatWest Car Loans
CAR
RAC
WITH A FREE RAC INSPECTION*
NatWest
The Action Bank
*Offer closes 15th September 1988

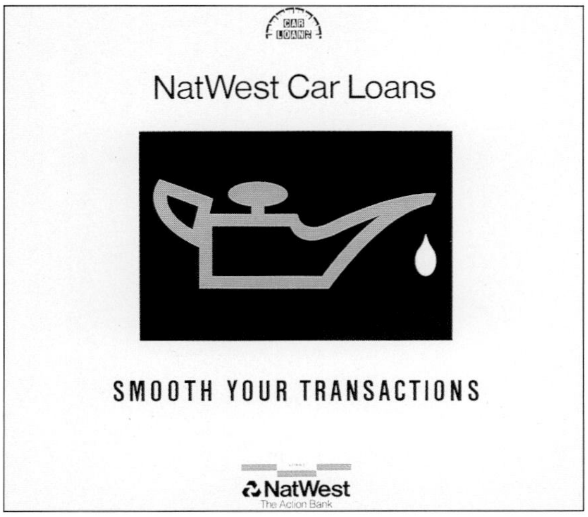

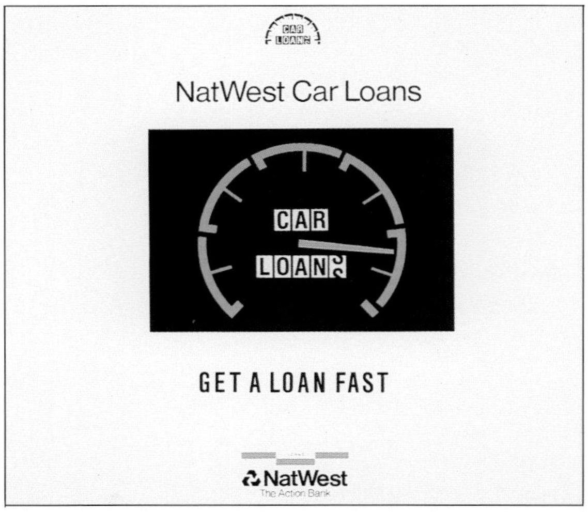

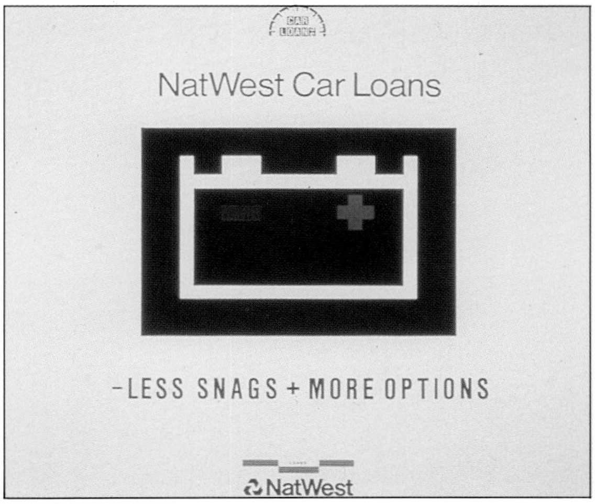

Natwest Car Loans

CLIENT: National Westminster Bank, London, UK
DESCRIPTION OF PRODUCT: 2ft × 2ft posters mounted on card for display
DESIGNER: Minale, Tattersfield & Partners Limited, Richmond, Surrey, UK
ILLUSTRATOR OR PHOTOGRAPHER: Minale Tattersfield
DATE OF COMPLETION: 1988
TARGET MARKET: Aimed at NatWest customers who may require a loan to buy a car
PLACE OF SALE: All NatWest branches
CLIENT'S BRIEF: To design a range of large posters that could be displayed within NatWest branches to support the brochures available on NatWest car loans
DESIGN RATIONALE: Key points in the NatWest Car Loans Brochure (also designed by MTP) are illustrated by familiar symbols taken from a car's dashboard. These adapt for large posters and panels.

Second Image Jeanswear

CLIENT: Second Image Limited, Greenford, Middlesex, UK

DESCRIPTION OF PRODUCT: Enamel wall signs/free standing (×2), jeanswear/denim display, shelf/counter stand

DESIGNER: Big-Active Limited, London, UK

DATE OF COMPLETION: 1989

TARGET MARKET: Basic jeanswear consumers (male & female) aged 15–35

PLACE OF SALE: Specialist jeanswear retailers/departments

CLIENT'S BRIEF: To develop a point-of-sale kit suitable for mailing. Flexibility and display of product were important considerations given the variety of in-store environments that the kit would have to work within.

DESIGN RATIONALE: The identity of the brand was animated over a series of items to evoke a sense of the display belonging to a bygone age. The story created gives a unique insight into the world projected by second image jeanswear.

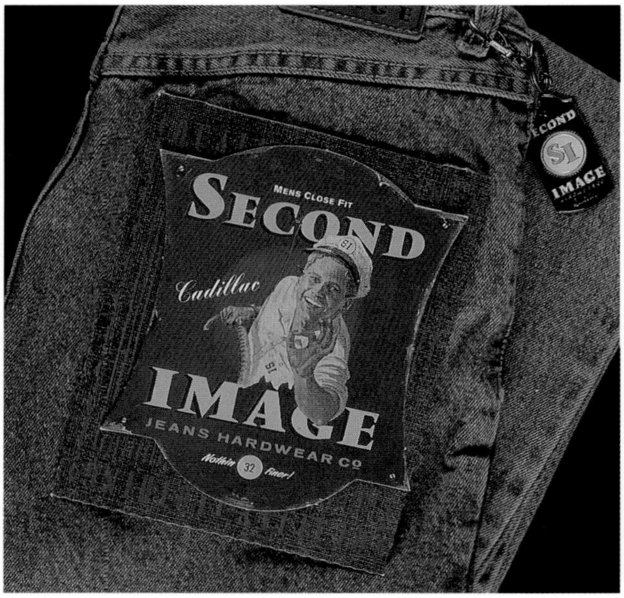

SI
SECOND IMAGE
SECOND IMAGE
JEANS HARDWEAR Co

Health & Beauty

CLIENT: Tesco Stores Ltd, Cheshunt, Hertfordshire, UK

DESCRIPTION OF PRODUCT: Hanging boards and display stand

DESIGNER: Andrew Kibble/Neil Hoye, Jones & Co Design Ltd, London, UK

ILLUSTRATOR OR PHOTOGRAPHER: Paul Kemp

DATE OF COMPLETION: Summer 1991

TARGET MARKET: People who shop at Tesco but normally buy health and beauty products at other pharmacies and chemists

PLACE OF SALE: Tesco superstores

CLIENT'S BRIEF: Identity and promotion was needed for the Health and Beauty department, encouraging the exploration by the customer of the area. It was also important to stimulate the purchase of a variety of products normally bought elsewhere, and to promote various brands within a scheme that suggested other purchases without detracting from the brand's impact.

DESIGN RATIONALE: It was decided to photograph the brands in their relevant situations but to heighten their impact by using only white and clear props. This reinforced the clean and fresh cosmetic appeal and allowed other products to stimulate purchase without detracting from the brand.

choose your free
health & beauty product here.
see leaflet for full details whilst stocks last.
offer closes 8th June 1991.
health
&
beauty
SURE
Plax
Gillette Sensor
FINESSE
SEVEN SEAS
macleans
NIVEA
Radox
HERBAL BATH

"K"

CLIENT: Garner Group, Bristol, UK

DESIGNER: Simpson Fitzherbert (SFB), London, UK

DATE OF COMPLETION: 1991

Rowenta Irons

CLIENT: Rowenta, Cambridge, Massachusetts, USA

DESCRIPTION OF PRODUCT: Iron

DESIGNER: Barry David Berger & Associates Inc, New York, USA

TARGET MARKET: High-end consumer

PLACE OF SALE: Department stores, speciality stores

CLIENT'S BRIEF: Irons are promoted at retail outlets by live demonstrations. The standard display mode is on-shelf. Department stores accept no client supplied displays so the designer must provide a display device that: appears high-end and compatible with product; provides detailed copy to differentiate up to six models; and is removable for live demonstrations; can be re-attached without hardware and tools; and can be permanently removed without residue so that display product is not lost for sale.

DESIGN RATIONALE: The injection moulding and hot-stamped plaque follows the only part of the iron that is common to all models; attaches with industrial-quality velcro and removable double-sided tape; allows left-or right-handed demonstrators to use the iron with or without the attached plaque; and requires little additional shelf space.

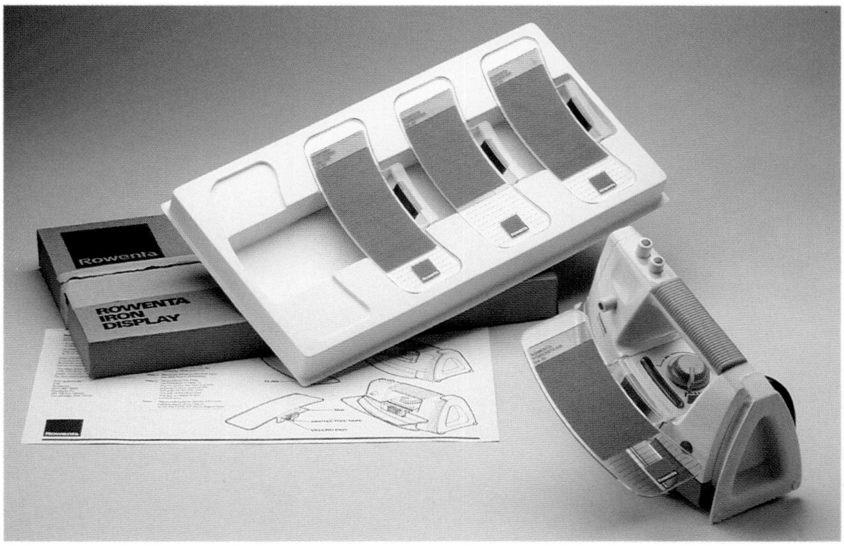

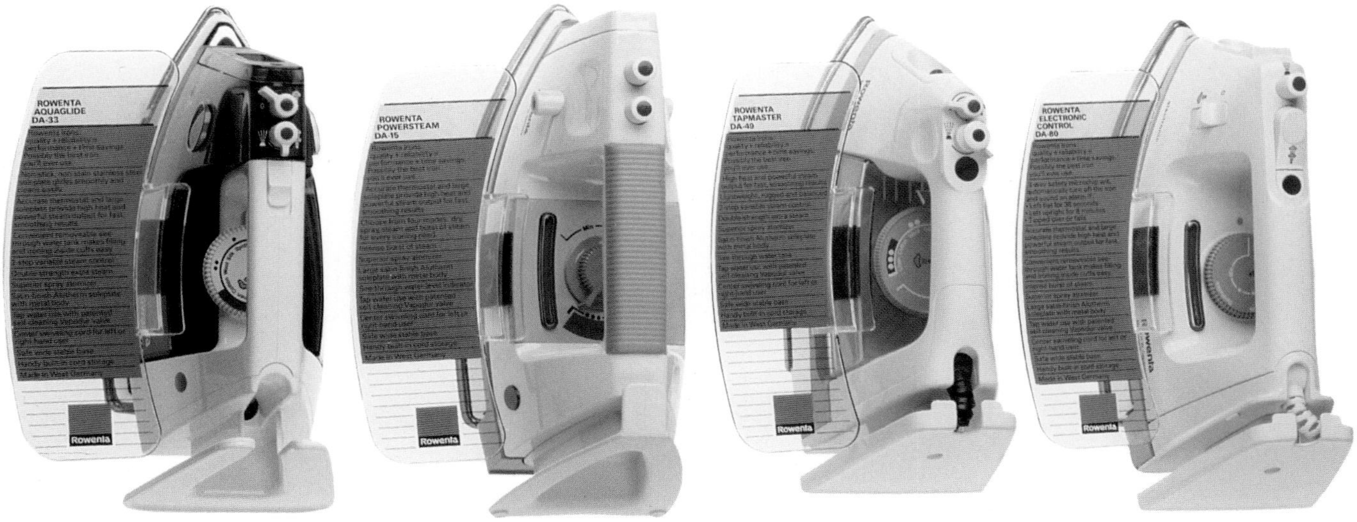

In-store systems The apotheosis of point of sale is the complete graphic treatment of an entire environment. During the retail boom of the 1980s design companies began to employ not only graphics and interior designers, but product designers, architects, space planners and even market researchers and retail analysts.

The design of a new store could include its name and corporate identity, its stationery, its ticketing and signage, its vans and head office, its shelving, carpets, lighting and interior ambience. And, of course, its point of sale. Graphics to promote product areas, special offers and sale items, were no longer simply hung from the ceiling, but could be incorporated into perimeter shelving, wall treatments and window displays. Price ticketing was designed to fit in with the overall colours and materials, graphic panels were held in place by specially designed fixtures that were not brought from shopfitters standard ranges. The result was a coordinated environment which supported the client's products and philosophy, and a dramatic reduction in clutter.

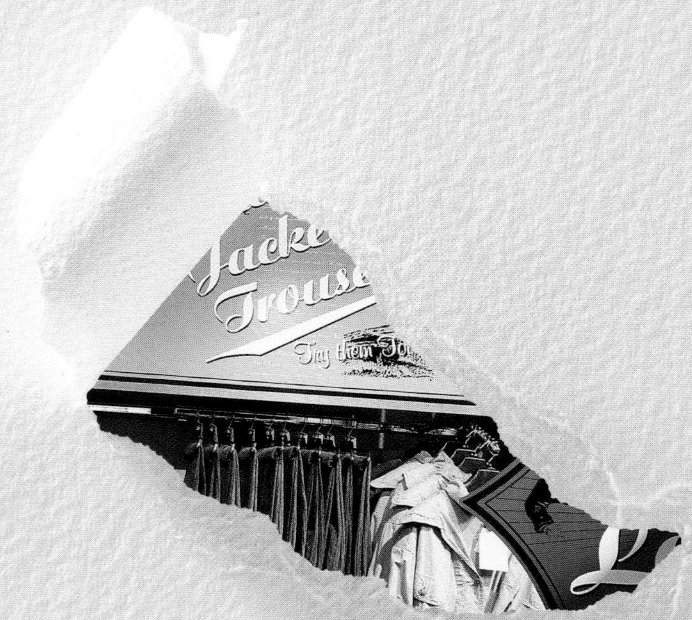

ground
EVEL
chart
compact discs
cassettes

Megastore

CLIENT: Virgin Retail Ltd, London, UK

DESCRIPTION OF PRODUCT: Adaptable merchandise system and signing

DESIGNER: 20/20 Design and Strategy Consultants, London, UK

PHOTOGRAPHER: Jon O'Brien

DATE OF COMPLETION: May 1990

TARGET MARKET: 17–40

PLACE OF SALE: Virgin Megastores (Retailer)

CLIENT'S BRIEF: To create a shopping environment which would be as exciting and adrenalin-pumping as the music itself, including merchandise display systems with an in-built adaptability – allowing for both day-to-day and long-term shifts in demand for different audio and video formats.

DESIGN RATIONALE: This was driven by three issues: 1) to ensure that the customer could quickly arrive at the product of their choice; 2) to give a merchandizing system that was completely flexible to dynamic day-to-day requirements and to new format presentation; 3) to inject every part of the megastore with an all-pervading uniqueness.

compact discs
rock and pop
rock & pop
aztec camera

The "Tower"

CLIENT: Virgin Retail Ltd, London, UK

DESCRIPTION OF PRODUCT: 30-ft high steel audio visual tower

DESIGNER: 20/20 Design and Strategy Consultants, London, UK

PHOTOGRAPHER: Jon OBrien

DATE OF COMPLETION: May 1990

TARGET MARKET: 17–40

PLACE OF SALE: Virgin Megastore (retailer)

CLIENT'S BRIEF: To create a dynamic and dramatic signal to attract customers onto the first floor.

DESIGN RATIONALE: Three requirements for the main entrance to the store were identified: 1) to create a focal point for directional signage; 2) to form a structure that would consolidate all the audio/visual technology in a space that could be kept uncluttered; 3) to illustrate in an exciting way there was much more above.

Chart Wall, Virgin Megastore

CLIENT: Virgin Retail Ltd, London, UK

DESIGNER: 20/20 Design & Strategy Consultants, London, UK

PHOTOGRAPHER: Jon O'Brien

DATE OF COMPLETION: July 1990

TARGET MARKET: Music and video customers, 25–40 years

PLACE OF SALE: Virgin Megastores

CLIENT'S BRIEF: Chart music still accounts for a large proportion of sales within the Megastores. Virgin wanted to develop a high-impact zone with a strong individual identity of its own, which would be dedicated to the display of these chart products – in all three formats (vinyl, CD and cassette).

DESIGN RATIONALE: The Chart Wall is located at the front of the store – a first port of call for the fast track shopper wishing to buy chart music. 20/20 used the same palette of materials used throughout the Megastore – but configured them in an individual way for the Chart Wall. This gives the area its individual identity, yet retains a link with the other departments in-store.

COMPUTER SOFTWARE
MACHINES
GAMES MACH
commodore 64
commodore 64
BATMAN
BATMAN

The "Android"

CLIENT: Virgin Retail Ltd, London, UK
DESCRIPTION OF PRODUCT: Three-legged interactive computer games presenter
DESIGNER: 20/20 Design and Strategy Consultants, London, UK
PHOTOGRAPHER: Jon O'Brien
DATE OF COMPLETION: December 1990
TARGET MARKET: 12–25
PLACE OF SALE: Virgin Games Centres (retailer)
CLIENT'S BRIEF: To demonstrate computer games in such a way that the customer can play the game but the shop assistant can control how long he or she plays for. The unit had to be dramatic and attention-grabbing as well as practical.
DESIGN RATIONALE: The prime consideration was to move away from any "amusement arcade" connotations yet encourage the target market to interact with the Android. We employed the design vernacular of computer games in space-age styling, providing the customer with a slice of environmental realism which mirrors the visual fantasy experienced through the screen.

The "Intelligent Wall"

CLIENT: Virgin Retail Ltd, London, UK
DESCRIPTION OF PRODUCT: Flexible, adaptable wall shelving system
DESIGNER: 20/20 Design and Strategy Consultants, London, UK
PHOTOGRAPHER: Jon O'Brien
DATE OF COMPLETION: December 1990
TARGET MARKET: 12–50
PLACE OF SALE: Virgin Games Centre (Retailer)
CLIENT'S BRIEF: To develop a wall shelving system that would be flexible enough to cope with a wide variety of different sized products and significant seasonal variation – particularly at Christmas.
DESIGN RATIONALE: The Intelligent Wall moves back and forth – and tilts. It expands and contracts to accommodate the required shelf depth, always keeping the merchandise in prime selling position and well presented. In addition, overhead graphic panels conceal storage compartments, enabling rapid replenishment of adjacent displays.

Dances with Wolves

CLIENT: Virgin Megastore, Paris, France

DESCRIPTION OF PRODUCT: Point-of-sale display unit

DESIGNER: Bruno Synave, Paris, France

DATE OF COMPLETION: February 1992

DESIGN RATIONALE: To interpret the point-of-sale material with the marketing concept so that it fitted the architecture of different sites.

7 OSCARS
DANSE AVEC LES LOUPS
CAISSES

DANSE AVEC LES LOUPS
UN FILM DE
KEVIN COSTNER
EN VIDEO
SORTIE

Levi's Young Men's Shirts

CLIENT: Levi Strauss & Co, San Francisco, CA

DESCRIPTION OF PRODUCT: Materials: MR 16, lighting. Pirelli flooring, Green plexi-glass, plywood

DESIGNER: Morla Design, Inc, San Francisco, CA

ILLUSTRATOR OR PHOTOGRAPHER: Jeanette Aramburu

DATE OF COMPLETION: January 1989

PLACE OF SALE: US department stores

DESIGN RATIONALE: This had minimal budget to effectively merchandize a new line of Levi shirts for young men. Construction techniques employed utilized 4ft × 8ft ½in edge-lit plexiglass with sand-blasted logo applied to surface. Corrugated aluminum, galvanized steel, and rubber tiling allowed for contemporary look with minimum expense.

Display Panels for In-store Presentation

CLIENT: Mothercare Ltd, London, UK

DESIGNER: RSCG Conran Design, London, UK

DATE OF COMPLETION: 1990

TARGET MARKET: Mothers of all ages

PLACE OF SALE: Mothercare retail outlets

CLIENT'S BRIEF: To create a sympathetic unified range of graphic material for all Mothercare outlets.

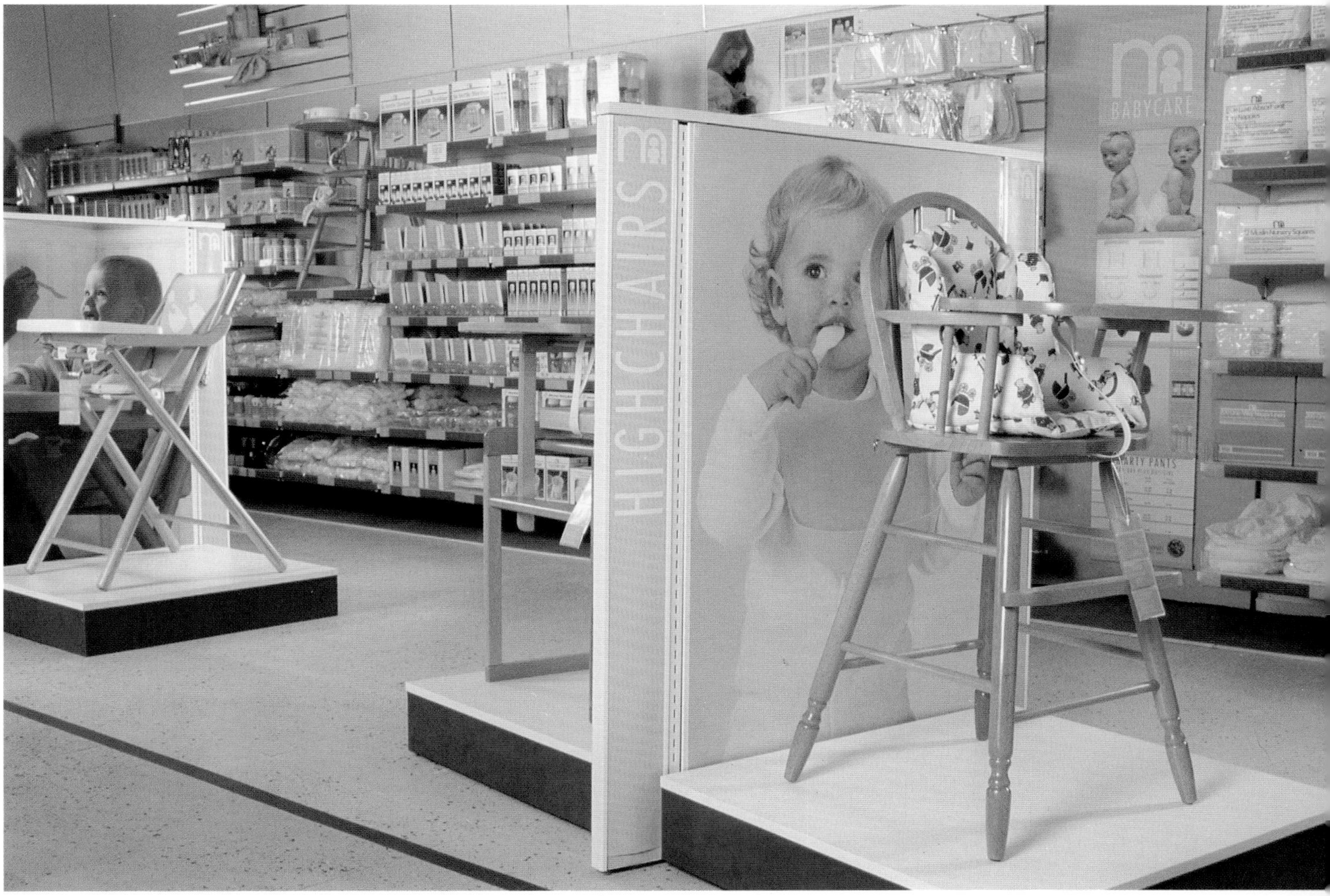

Levi's

Levi Jeans

DESCRIPTION OF PRODUCT: Exhibition for Levi jeans

CLIENT: Levi-Strauss, San Francisco, USA

DESIGNER: Checkland Kindleysides, Leicester, UK

Clothing & Household Linen

CLIENT: Hema, The Netherlands

DESIGNER: Davies & Baron, London, UK

DATE OF COMPLETION: November 1990

TARGET MARKET: Mass market retailing

CLIENT'S BRIEF: Hema is a Dutch variety store that has around 1500 different own-brand products. Davies & Baron's brief for the signage was to create atmosphere within product areas while retaining an overall homogeneous style. Therefore, illustrations were commissioned from Colin Barnes and combined with a bold typographic style.

Herenmode

Kindermode

Top Man/Portfolio

CLIENT: Top Man, London, UK

DESCRIPTION OF PRODUCT: Menswear

DESIGNER: Davies & Baron, London, UK

DATE OF COMPLETION: 1989

PLACE OF SALE: Top Man outlets throughout the UK

CLIENT'S BRIEF: Top Man asked Davies & Baron to determine each one of the key clothing areas within its shops. The Davies & Baron graphics team, drawing influence from 1950s Americana, helped to segment the plethora of offers within Top Man.

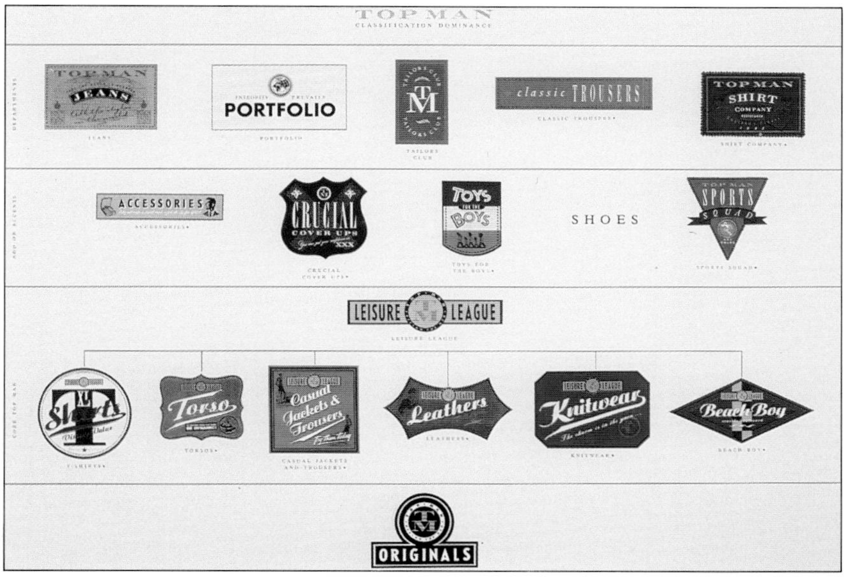
TOP MAN
CLASSIFICATION DOMINANCE
TOP MAN JEANS
PORTFOLIO
classic TROUSERS
TOP MAN SHIRT COMPANY
ACCESSORIES
CRUCIAL COVER-UPS
TOYS FOR THE BOYS
SHOES
SPORTS SQUAD
LEISURE LEAGUE
Torso
Casual Jackets & Trousers
Leathers
Knitwear
Beach Boy
ORIGINALS

Levi's
PEPE
EASY
Lee
TOP MAN
JEANS
All the styles in the world

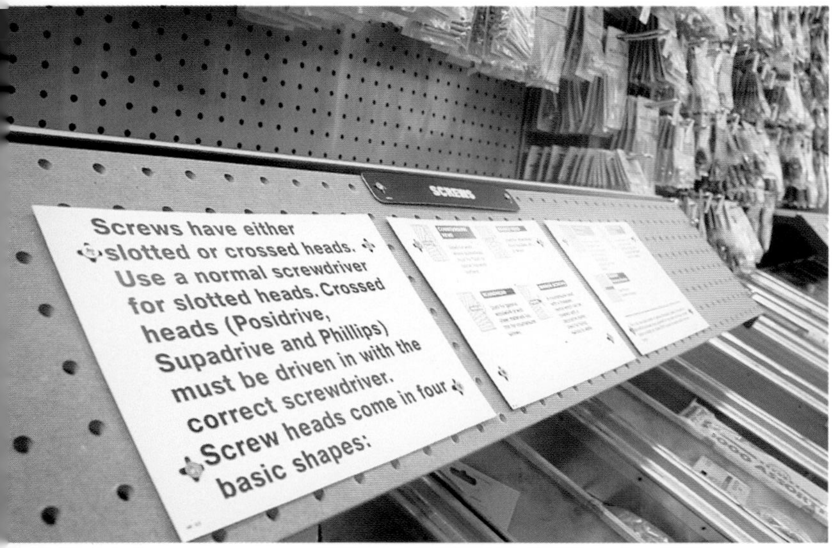

Do-it-all Stores

CLIENT: W H Smith, London, UK

DESIGNER: RSCG Conran Design, London, UK

DATE OF COMPLETION: 1989

TARGET MARKET: Customers, predominantly male, interested in DIY

PLACE OF SALE: Do-it-all stores in the UK.

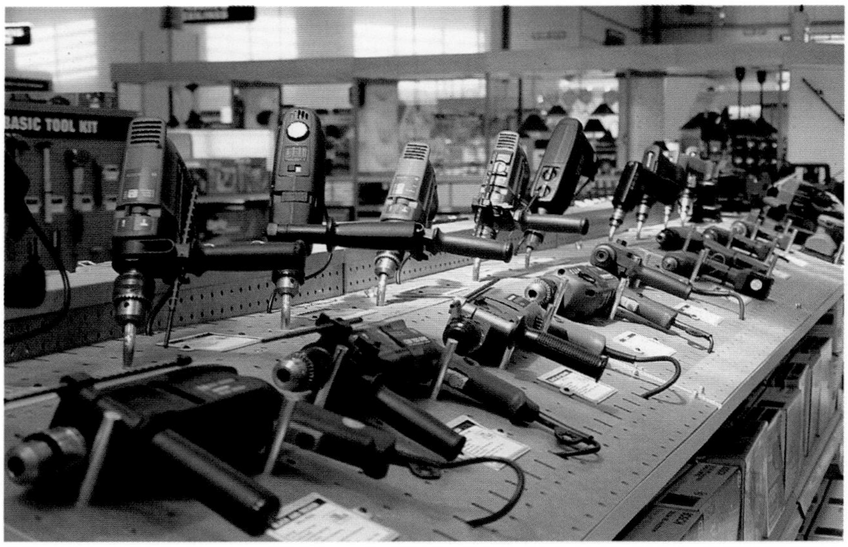

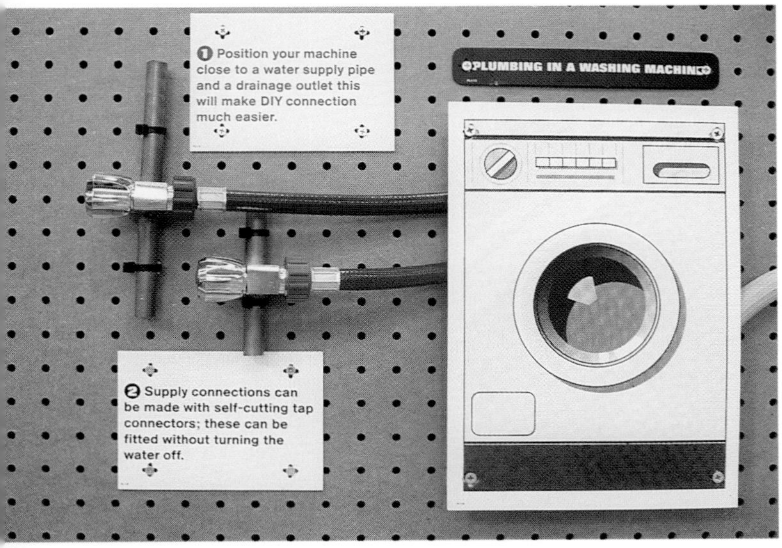
1 Position your machine close to a water supply pipe and a drainage outlet this will make DIY connection much easier.
PLUMBING IN A WASHING MACHINE
2 Supply connections can be made with self-cutting tap connectors; these can be fitted without turning the water off.

COMMON PLUMBING JOBS MADE EASY
FITTING AN OUTSIDE TAP

WALL FIXINGS
DOORS
FIRE EXIT
FIRE PREVENTION

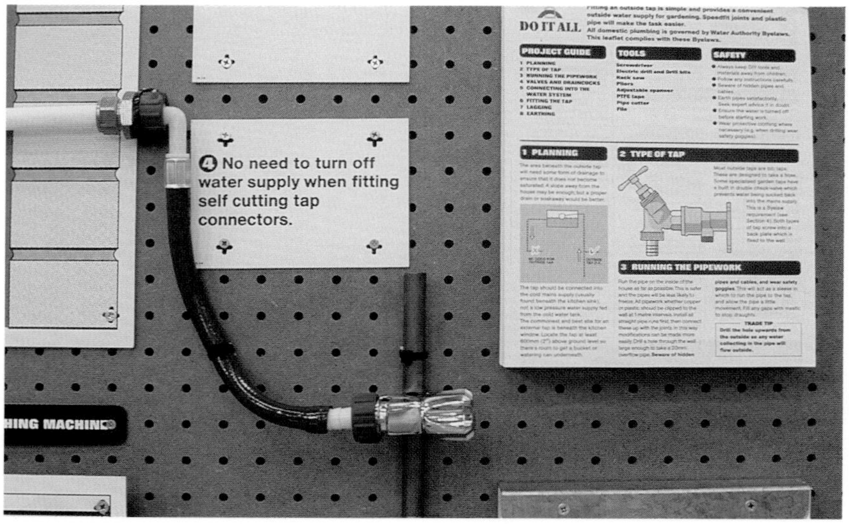
4 No need to turn off water supply when fitting self cutting tap connectors.
DO IT ALL
PROJECT GUIDE
TOOLS
SAFETY
1 PLANNING
2 TYPE OF TAP
3 RUNNING THE PIPEWORK
TRADE TIP

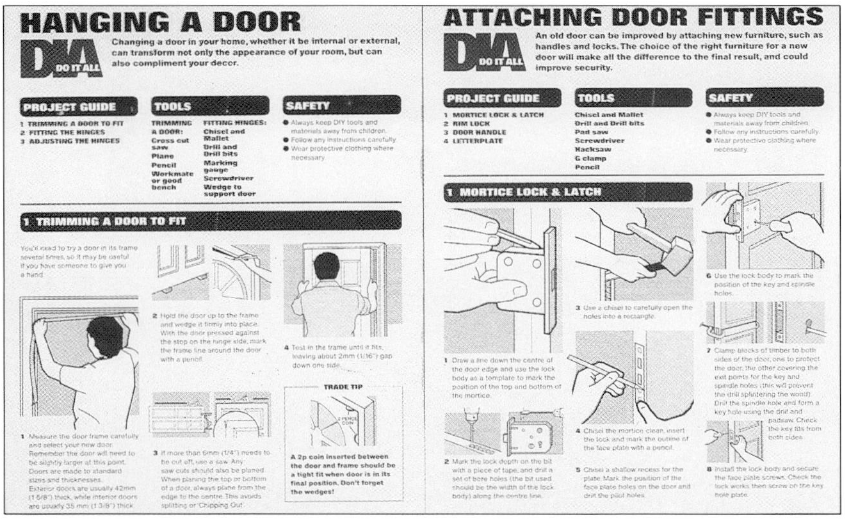

HANGING A DOOR

DO IT ALL

Changing a door in your home, whether it be internal or external, can transform not only the appearance of your room, but can also compliment your decor.

PROJECT GUIDE

1 TRIMMING A DOOR TO FIT
2 FITTING THE HINGES
3 ADJUSTING THE HINGES

TOOLS

TRIMMING A DOOR:
Cross cut saw
Plane
Pencil
Workmate or good bench

FITTING HINGES:
Chisel and Mallet
Drill and Drill bits
Marking gauge
Screwdriver
Wedge to support door

SAFETY

- Always keep DIY tools and materials away from children.
- Follow any instructions carefully
- Wear protective clothing where necessary

1 TRIMMING A DOOR TO FIT

You'll need to try a door in its frame several times, so it may be useful if you have someone to give you a hand.

1 Measure the door frame carefully and select your new door. Remember the door will need to be slightly larger at this point. Doors are made to standard sizes and thicknesses. Exterior doors are usually 42mm (1 5/8") thick, while interior doors are usually 35 mm (1 3/8") thick.

2 Hold the door up to the frame and wedge it firmly into place. With the door pressed against the stop on the hinge side, mark the frame line around the door with a pencil.

3 If more than 6mm (1/4") needs to be cut off, use a saw. Any saw cuts should also be planed. When planing the top or bottom of a door, always plane from the edge to the centre. This avoids splitting or 'Chipping Out'.

4 Test in the frame until it fits, leaving about 2mm (1/16") gap down one side.

TRADE TIP

2 PENCE COIN

A 2p coin inserted between the door and frame should be a tight fit when door is in its final position. Don't forget the wedges!

ATTACHING DOOR FITTINGS

DO IT ALL

An old door can be improved by attaching new furniture, such as handles and locks. The choice of the right furniture for a new door will make all the difference to the final result, and could improve security.

PROJECT GUIDE

1 MORTICE LOCK & LATCH
2 RIM LOCK
3 DOOR HANDLE
4 LETTERPLATE

TOOLS

Chisel and Mallet
Drill and Drill bits
Pad saw
Screwdriver
Hacksaw
G clamp
Pencil

SAFETY

- Always keep DIY tools and materials away from children.
- Follow any instructions carefully.
- Wear protective clothing where necessary.

1 MORTICE LOCK & LATCH

1 Draw a line down the centre of the door edge and use the lock body as a template to mark the position of the top and bottom of the mortice.

2 Mark the lock depth on the bit with a piece of tape, and drill a set of bore holes (the bit used should be the width of the lock body) along the centre line.

3 Use a chisel to carefully open the holes into a rectangle.

4 Chisel the mortice clean, insert the lock and mark the outline of the face plate with a pencil.

5 Chisel a shallow recess for the plate. Mark the position of the face plate holes on the door and drill the pilot holes.

6 Use the lock body to mark the position of the key and spindle holes.

7 Clamp blocks of timber to both sides of the door, one to protect the door, the other covering the exit points for the key and spindle holes (this will prevent the drill splintering the wood). Drill the spindle hole and form a key hole using the drill and padsaw. Check the key fits from both sides.

8 Install the lock body and secure the face plate screws. Check the lock works then screw on the key hole plate.

Image Wall

CLIENT: Porsche Cars Great Britain Ltd, Reading, Berks, UK

DESCRIPTION OF PRODUCT: A series of 2-m high, modular panels manufactured from heat-formed foamex which can be configured in various combinations to form point-of-sale displays.

DESIGNER: John Furneaux, Furneaux Stewart Design & Communication, London, UK

PHOTOGRAPHER: Nicholas Gentilli

DATE OF COMPLETION: 1989

TARGET MARKET: Official Porsche Centre customers

PLACE OF SALE: Official Porsche Centre Network (dealership network) in Great Britain and worldwide

CLIENT'S BRIEF: To design a complete point-of-sale system, which would enhance product presentation, convey and make available knowledge of the Porsche product and therefore increase sales in the showroom.

DESIGN RATIONALE: The brief called for a semi-permanent yet inherently flexible design solution. The system needed to be sufficiently permanent to ensure that the client's products, services and corporate identity were correctly and consistently displayed, yet flexible enough to perform as space divider or pure point-of-sale system whenever required.

PORSCHE

PORSCHE

Cosmetics
& Fragrances
Cosmetics
& Fragrances
Skin Care
Hair Accessories
Pharmacy

John Bell & Croyden

CLIENT: McCarthy plc, Leighton Buzzard, Bedfordshire, UK

DESCRIPTION OF PRODUCT: Comprehensive redesign and refurbishment of a flagship health-care department store servicing health-care professionals as well as retailing to the general public.

DESIGNER: XMPR International, London, UK

DATE OF COMPLETION: July 1989

TARGET MARKET: Health-care professionals, prescription and over-the-counter purchasers, and specialist and general pharmacy buyers.

CLIENT'S BRIEF: The objective was to help re-establish John Bell and Croyden as a leading market authority in the health-care sector. The project demanded a complete overhaul of all aspects of the interior and exterior of this prestigious site and the introduction of effective space management, customer circulation, merchandizing, display, lighting and signage systems.

DESIGN RATIONALE: The project commenced with a thorough planning and merchandizing analysis to ensure departments could be relocated and allotted space based upon potential revenue. A walkway was introduced to assist customer flows and merchandizing systems, and concessions were rationalized to evoke a stronger store personality.

Sony Centre

CLIENT: Sony Europa GmbH, Cologne, Germany

DESCRIPTION OF PRODUCT: The Sony Centre is a specialist, authorized dealership retailing exclusively Sony products across Europe

DESIGNER: XMPR International, London, UK

DATE OF COMPLETION: April 1992

TARGET MARKET: Mainstream consumers seeking the same brand values inherent in the Sony brand – quality, attention to detail, and performance.

PLACE OF SALE: Sony Centres have already been introduced in Switzerland and the Netherlands, and are planned for other markets across Europe.

CLIENT'S BRIEF: To create a branded, aspirational retail offer exclusively merchandizing Sony consumer products. The scope of the project includes naming, visual identity, all aspects of merchandizing, point-of-sale, lighting and display, application to stand alone and shop-in-shop locations and the development of a European design manual.

DESIGN RATIONALE: The design scheme is, in essence, an extension of the Sony brand. The merchandizing system is extremely flexible and designed to direct attention primarily on to the product. Quality finishes, attention to detail and careful cable management avoid clutter and create a crisp environment.

SONY
SONY
SONY
CHANGE

SONY
SONY

NOVITÀ
DAVID LEAVITT
EGUALI AMORI

Sting
Biblioteq

Biblioteq
Biblioteq

Biblioteq
Biblioteq

In-store Graphics

CLIENT: Mondadori Group, Milan, Italy

DESIGNER: Fran Lane, Landor Associates, London, UK

ILLUSTRATOR OR PHOTOGRAPHER: Jeff Fisher

DATE OF COMPLETION: Summer 1990

TARGET MARKET: Italian youth market: to encourage book purchase

PLACE OF SALE: Book shop owned by publishers

CLIENT'S BRIEF: To produce a new concept in book shop design and promotion that encouraged sale of books among Italian youth. To be positioned well away from the cold, serious and academic stance of existing book retailers.

DESIGN RATIONALE: The retail identity was kept deliberately classic and timeless to avoid change. It reflects the use of all the human senses in an environment that is warm, stimulating and fun. Retail point-of-sale graphics are highly visual and produced economically in order to be changed regularly.

Part of the promotion designed by Fran Lane for Mondadori's own bookshop to encourage young Italians to buy books.

Libri
Video
Quotidiani
Fotografia
Musica
Teatro
Regali
Novità

Index of Products